THE MACMILLAN
BASEBALL

Quiz Book

COMPILED FROM THE BASEBALL ENCYCLOPEDIA® BY
Scott Flatow and Ken Samelson

Macmillan • USA

Macmillan
A Simon & Schuster Macmillan Company
1633 Broadway
New York, NY 10019

Library of Congress Cataloging-in-Publication Data

The Macmillan baseball quiz book / compiled by Scott Flatow
and Ken Samelson
     p. cm.
     ISBN: 0-02-861594-8
     1. Baseball--United States--Miscellanea.
     I. Flatow, Scott 1966-   II. Samelson, Ken 1958-
GV867.3.M33 1997
796.357'0973—dc21   97-5649
                                                CIP

Manufactured in the United States of America
10 9 8 7 6 5 4 3 2 1

Book Design by Kris Tobiassen

Contents

Acknowledgments

S everal people lent their talents to this effort. Three of the most knowledgeable baseball aficionados, all esteemed members of the Society for American Baseball Research (SABR), were asked to read the manuscript. David Nemec, author of several top baseball quiz books of his own, checked the accuracy of the material and made many valuable suggestions. Dick Thompson, one of the leading biographical researchers of ballplayers, not only scanned the text, but shared many of his own questions. Al Blumkin offered his extensive knowledge of every facet of baseball as well as an unmatched eye for detail.

We would also like to extend our appreciation to production editor Chris Dreyer, copyeditor Maria Massey, and proofreader Denise Hawkins Coursey, all of whom have now absorbed more baseball trivia than they ever cared to know. Thanks for keeping us on the right track. Dick Corey's technical wizardry and infinite patience bailed us out of more than one jam, and Seiji Ogata picked up his share of "saves" as well.

Finally, we wish to thank Anna Duneghy and Liz Samelson for their continued encouragement and support.

Introduction

Baseball and trivia go hand in hand. Whether sitting at a game or in a bar, you have heard fans firing questions back and forth. Maybe you're one of them. Now with *The Macmillan Baseball Quiz Book*, you can arm yourself with facts that will stump even the most knowledgeable baseball expert.

With the publication of *The Baseball Encyclopedia*® in 1969, followers of our National Pastime had vast amounts of information, previously unavailable, at their fingertips. Devotees could explore the game in greater depth while making their own discoveries.

This book is a result of that landmark work and its nine subsequent editions. Many of the unique questions found here come from years of scouring the fact-filled pages of the *Encyclopedia*. The questions cover events from the formation of the National Association in 1871 through the 1996 World Series.

The categories are organized according to the chapters in *The Baseball Encyclopedia*®. Each section addresses a broad spectrum of highlights from baseball's rich history. Who was the only man to win a Most Valuable Player award whose career ended before he turned thirty? Readers will find him in Chapter Two, "Special Achievements." This fierce competitor won more games than any other pitcher who never played for a New York team. Look for this question in Chapter Three, "All-Time Leaders." In Chapter Five, "The Teams and Their Players," learn the name of the man who is the only regular player on a twentieth century pennant winner to bat under .200 in 400 at-bats. Chapter Nine, "Trades," includes the 300-game winner who retired without reporting after being dealt to the New York Yankees.

Whether the reader is a diligent student of nineteenth century play or an avid fan of the current scene, we cover all the bases. So, step right up to the plate and start swinging. No matter how familiar you are with the game and its history, you will come away knowing more than before.

NOTE: All questions are current as of January 1, 1997.

CHAPTER ONE

History of Baseball

1. Which member of the New York Knickerbocker Club published the baseball rule book that greatly increased the game's popularity?
2. Another baseball pioneer was this intrepid reporter who created the box score and wrote a history of the game in 1867.
3. Boston received this colorful position player of the 1880s for $10,000, a staggering amount for that time.
4. Name the star player and lawyer who spearheaded the creation of the Players' League in 1890.
5. What was the original name of the American League?
6. The Negro National League was the brainchild of which African American Hall of Famer?
7. The Baseball Hall of Fame formally opened its doors in what year?
8. This New York Giant outfielder filed a suit against Commissioner Happy Chandler in reaction to the blacklisting of Mexican League jumpers who attempted to return to the majors.

9. His contract with Houston made him the first million-dollar-per-year player in salary.

10. Name the Milwaukee Brewers' owner who stepped in as acting commissioner upon Fay Vincent's resignation.

CHAPTER TWO

Special Achievements

1. The only Most Valuable Player (MVP) whose career was over before he turned thirty is familiar with prison bars.
2. The first position player to win a World Series MVP drove home 12 Series runs in a losing cause.
3. He has the distinction of being the only World Series MVP to begin the season with a different team.
4. The only position player to win an MVP without hitting a homer fanned only 13 times in a league-leading 624 at-bats.
5. Which Rookie of the Year won the award after playing for two other teams?
6. Prior to being the A.L. Rookie of the Year, this man played in the N.L. with the Padres.
7. Which Rookie of the Year spent his entire nineteen-year career with one team?
8. In 1957 *The Sporting News* named its first Gold Glove winners. The three outfielders selected were drawn from both leagues. Name this trio.

9. Who failed to win the MVP in either of his two Triple Crown seasons?

10. In 1962, he became the first former Rookie of the Year elected to the Hall of Fame.

11. Major hype accompanied this Rookie of the Year's sophomore flop. After 201 games his career was over, the fewest games by a former position-playing honoree.

12. After garnering the Cy Young Award in 1980, he appeared in only 15 more games.

13. Of all the players who broke in to the majors since the inception of the Cy Young Award, his five 20-win seasons are the most by any man who never received the award.

14. He won the 1965 N.L. Rookie of the Year with a .250 batting average. The player who finished a distant second in the balloting is in the Hall of Fame. Name these two players.

15. Few will remember the first man elected to the Hall of Fame as a player whose primary position was behind the mask.

16. Since the origin of the Manager of the Year Award in 1983, who was the first skipper to win the award with two different teams in the same league?

17. The only player to win a Gold Glove in the fifties, sixties, and seventies was this shortstop.

18. Name the Pirate who snapped Ozzie Smith's streak of consecutive Gold Gloves at thirteen in 1993?

19. Other than Johnny Bench, only one other N.L. catcher was honored with a Gold Glove during the 1970s. Name this man, who has seen both his father and his son play in the bigs.

20. A cat off the mound, he is the only pitcher to bag the Gold Glove in both leagues.

21. It was this native of Mexico who halted Brooks Robinson's streak of sixteen straight Gold Gloves in 1976.

22. Which two players earned the baseball writers' MVP Award and its predecessor, the League Award?

23. This first baseman voluntarily ended his playing streak at 822 games to attend his mother's funeral in 1937.

24. His only victory of 1945 after coming back from the war was a no-hitter for the Philadelphia Athletics to defeat the Browns on September 9.

25. A month prior to his older sibling throwing a no-hitter to beat Florida, this brother lost a perfect game against Montreal in the tenth inning. Name the two hurlers.

26. Before Barry Larkin in 1995, who was the last shortstop in the senior circuit to win the MVP?

27. This Cy Young winner's real first name is Dewey. Can you name him?

28. Two years prior to securing the Cy Young as a reliever, this player set a major league record when he failed to complete any of his 37 starting assignments.

29. The first man to hurl a no-hitter in a game that he did not have to bat in turned the same trick the following year.

30. Which Cy Young recipient was the first man this century to walk at least 175 batters in two straight seasons?

31. This first player to club as many as 47 homers in a season and who was born outside of the United States also earned an MVP the same season he led the league in dingers.

32. He hurled a complete game no-hitter for a pennant-winning team yet was not called upon in the Fall Classic because he was outclassed by Plank, Bender, and Coakley. Name this player.

33. Who had the shortest tenure as Commissioner of Baseball?

34. This righty threw a ten-inning complete game no-hitter two months after he lost a no-hit bid in the eleventh inning in 1965.

35. Which Rookie of the Year was the last freshman pitcher to record twenty or more complete games?

36. At nineteen he became the youngest player to win the Rookie of the Year Award.

37. Both leagues' Rookies of the Year for 1970 were no longer living by 1983. Name them.

38. Name the two Rookies of the Year who later managed World Championship teams.

39. This Rookie of the Year stole over 100 bases the year he won the award and in each of the two following seasons.

40. The only 20-game winner to win the Rookie of the Year Award finished up his career in 1962 with 61 career victories.

41. Which Rookie of the Year and MVP winner had a twin brother who played in the majors?

42. Many solid seasons followed for this Rookie of the Year who also won the batting crown during that campaign.

43. Fenway faithful thrilled to the season when he took home both Rookie and MVP honors.

44. Tommy Lasorda bled Dodger blue when this guy picked up the Rookie of the Year and the Cy Young awards.

45. Besides Dwight Gooden's record-breaking 276 strikeouts in 1984, three other Rookie of the Year winners fanned 200 or more. They did it exactly twenty years apart in 1955, 1975, and 1995. Name the three players.

46. At 5'5" this diminutive Washington outfielder is the shortest man to win Rookie of the Year.

47. Excluding Negro League stars, whose careers were delayed because of racial barriers, the oldest player to win Rookie of the Year was the 1957 honoree, who also led N.L. hurlers in strikeouts.

48. After winning the Rookie of the Year Award, he played only one more season before he was killed in an off-season accident.

49. The two men who were awarded their respective league's MVP in 1994 were both born on May 27, 1968. Can you name these titans?

50. Only one pitcher-catcher battery finished 1–2 in the MVP race. The pitcher won 25 games more than he lost, and the receiver whacked 25 homers. Name this duo.

51. Who is the only outfielder to play in 1,000 or more consecutive games?

52. Who voluntarily retired after a Cy Young-winning season?

53. This MVP led the N.L. in ribbies and batting but still fell 24 dingers shy of tying Willie Stargell for the league lead.

54. Two years before he became the first lefty to toss a perfect game in the A.L., he led the junior circuit in relief appearances with 81.

55. Name the first man elected to the Hall of Fame who batted as a DH.

56. Which pitcher fashioned a perfect game in his team's first season in its new location?

57. This lanky 6'7" chucker tossed a perfect game on the last day of the 1984 season.

58. From the "Where are they now?" file comes this righty who never won another game after spinning a no-hitter for the White Sox in 1986.

59. Louisville of the American Association was the first team to feature no-hitters by two pitchers in 1882. Who were they?

60. On October 2, 1972, he threw the second no-hitter of his career. It also happened to be the first no-hitter that occurred outside the United States.

61. Death came at an early age to this Cleveland twirler, who is the only man to pitch both a no-hitter and a perfect game against the same team.

62. Jim Abbott threw a no-hitter despite missing one hand and received national recognition for his feat. However, another one-handed hurler threw a no-hitter for Cleveland back in 1883. Name him.

63. June 29, 1990, was the day that these two hurlers toiling for West Coast teams spun no-hitters in separate games.

64. One of the game's early big winners who threw from the left side was this man who completed no-hitters both before and after the mound was moved to its current distance from the plate.

65. Which Hall of Famer had a perfect game to his credit before he turned twenty-one?

66. Playing shortstop, this player hit 1 homer, drove in 47 runs, and fanned 124 times, yet those marks were enough to capture the A.L. Rookie of the Year in 1992.

67. The Arch Ward Memorial Award is given to the player who stands out in which contest?

68. He won the N.L. Cy Young even though he began the season in the A.L.

69. This playboy was the first pitcher to fashion a no-hitter for an expansion team in its inaugural season.

70. Although better known for his thundering bat, he was the only A.L. first baseman to win a Gold Glove during the 1985 to 1994 seasons other than Don Mattingly.

71. Keith Hernandez's streak of eleven straight Gold Gloves was halted by this man in 1989.

72. One of the game's undisputed greats was the only man to win the Chalmers and League MVP awards.

73. What percent of the vote does a player currently need to be elected to the Hall of Fame by the baseball writers?

74. He died a year after winning the World Series MVP Award.

75. The first man to win an MVP while playing for a team who finished below .500 accomplished the same feat the following season.

76. Name the former A.L. president for whom the American League Championship series MVP is named.

77. He ruled with an iron fist as Commissioner of Baseball for a record twenty-four years until his death in 1944.

78. Two years before he became the first Cy Young winner for a team with a losing record, he was the unanimous selection for the same award on a pennant-winning team.

79. This speed demon and former MVP is the only player to retire with over 2,000 hits and fewer than 500 RBI.

80. A year after the pitching half of this brother duo won the MVP, the catching half and fellow teammate finished second to Stan Musial in the balloting for MVP.

81. Name the first National League player to win Rookie of the Year at shortstop.

82. Between 1931 and 1963 only one N.L. hot cornerman won the MVP. Who is he?

83. Who won the first MVP Award for an expansion team?

84. After eighteen seasons, this player won his first and only MVP.

85. He has the distinction of winning MVP awards in consecutive seasons while playing for different teams.

86. Two players have won the MVP at two different positions. Name them.

87. Yogi Berra and Roy Campanella each won three MVP awards during the fifties. But do you know the name of the catcher who snagged three Gold Gloves during the same decade?

88. The only no-hitter of 1957 was fired by a pitcher who was already closing in on thirty-three when he broke in to the majors four years earlier.

89. Until his perfect game in 1964, the Phillies had not had a complete game no-hitter in a record fifty-eight years.

90. None of Cincinnati's heavy hitters could keep these two hurlers from throwing no-hitters against the Reds at Riverfront Stadium only twenty days apart in June 1971.

91. Despite hitting more than 50 homers twice, he never won an MVP.

92. Forty-nine homers, 165 RBI, and a .363 average were his Triple Crown winning numbers in 1934. Unfortunately, in the heavy-hitting thirties, these marks were only good enough for fifth place in the MVP balloting that year.

93. Knocking 58 out of the park in 1938 wasn't enough to earn this man an MVP.

94. In 1940 he clocked 43 homers with 137 RBI. Seven years later he clubbed 51 homers and had 138 RBI. Even though all of these totals led his league, this player never won an MVP.

95. This Kansas City Royal hit .312 and drove in 112 runs but finished second behind Rod Carew in the MVP race of 1977. In thirteen seasons this player never received another MVP vote.

96. Name the Philadelphia outfielder who finished second in the MVP voting to Joe Morgan in 1975 and second to George Foster in 1977 despite driving in 120 runs the first time and 130 the second.

97. Johnny Bench's numbers in 1970 and 1972 forced this Hall of Fame outfielder into the MVP runner-up spot both years.

98. His 230 hits and 153 RBI placed him third in his league's MVP race of 1962.

99. Mickey Mantle drove his last major league homer off the man who won the Cy Young the previous year. Name the pitcher.

100. He finished second to Hideo Nomo for the 1995 N.L. Rookie of the Year Award and helped lead his team to a World Championship.

101. This moundsman won two Gold Gloves as a veteran, one at age thirty-six and the other at thirty-eight, in 1985 and 1987 respectively.

102. In 1984 this Mariner fanned over 200 batters. He lost the Rookie of the Year Award to his teammate, who won the honor with 27 homers and 116 RBI. Name this pair.

103. Name the American League third sacker who won Gold Gloves at that position in each of the first three seasons the award was handed out.

104. This N.L. rookie catcher quietly captured a Gold Glove in 1995.

105. Stationed at second when he won the Rookie of the Year Award, this player later won a pair of Gold Gloves in the outfield.

106. In 1962 they formed the first teammate battery to win the Gold Glove.

107. Who was the first reigning Cy Young winner to switch teams during the off-season?

108. As a result of Jackie Robinson's rookie accomplishments, this chucker's 21–5 effort went unrewarded.

109. As a rookie Vince Coleman kept this freshman 20-game winner in the shadows during the 1985 season.

110. He won Rookie of the Year at first base and was a teammate of the man who had received the honor the previous year with the same club, at the same position. Name this pair.

111. This New York Giant threw nine no-hit innings only to see it broken up in the tenth during his team's 1909 opener.

112. Of all the players who broke in to the majors since 1956, it took this man the most seasons to win a Cy Young.

113. There is one team that has existed throughout the Rookie of the Year Award's history but has never had a team member win the award. Which club?

114. A 1.65 ERA accompanied the first man to win a Cy Young with an expansion team.

115. Puerto Rico was the birthplace of this Cy Young honoree.

116. Winning the rookie award was just the beginning for this pitcher who later grabbed three Cy Youngs.

117. In 1956 this shortstop played 142 games with 520 at-bats but failed to homer or steal a base. Four years later he won a batting crown and his league's MVP.

118. Mark McGwire's 49 homers proved too much for this other rookie, who paced the A.L. with 207 hits in 1987.

119. Boston and Brooklyn were both held hitless in consecutive starts by this "Dutch Master."

120. Who won the Triple Crown in the first season of the American League's existence as a major league?

121. Five years after his Triple Crown achievement, this player hit only 4 homers in 554 at-bats in 1942.

122. In 1933 two men played in the same city and won the Triple Crown in their respective leagues. The A.L. player's club finished 19 games out of first place and the National Leaguer's outfit landed 31 games off the pace.

123. Who is the only switch-hitter to win the Triple Crown?

124. Eddie Collins, Tris Speaker, and Sam Crawford finished second to this player in batting, homers, and RBI respectively the year he won the Triple Crown.

125. A graduate of West Point, this Commissioner received a lot of flak when he failed to cancel games after the assasinations of Martin Luther King Jr. and Robert Kennedy in 1968.

126. In 1884 this Cincinnati player hurled a no-hitter in the Union Association and led the league in triples.

127. They haven't had a no-hit game pitched against them since 1958. Name the team and the pitcher who last victimized them.

128. In 1993 this expansion team logged its ninth no-hitter. Its opponent was another expansion crew that has been around as long as it has but has never fashioned a no-hitter. Name these teams of extremes.

129. The man who held the record for the most consecutive games played at shortstop prior to Cal Ripken also competed in all 27 World Series games his teams played while he was active.

130. A Cy Young was awarded to this hurler whose team played at a .378 clip.

131. Cap Anson's Chicago club had the first pitcher to deliver 3 no-hit games during the 1880s.

132. Between 1971 and 1975 George Scott was the A.L. Gold Glove at first. However, the last man to win it before and the first man after Scott happens to be the same player.

133. Lethal moves to first and a sky-high leg kick were signatures of the first lefty to win the Cy Young.

134. It has been around since long before the creation of the Cy Young, yet this team has never numbered a winner among its ranks.

135. Stationed exclusively at first as Rookie of the Year, this player switched to second during his sophomore season. He would play only 48 more games at his initial position during the rest of his career.

136. This Houston pitcher's throwing error allowed Pete Rose to reach base and eventually score the run that beat him, despite pitching a complete game no-hitter in 1964.

137. By the time he was twenty-five this player had already bagged two Cy Young honors. Seven years later he was nursing a bad wing that shelved him throughout 1996.

138. Two men have won Cy Young awards while in their second tour of duty with a team. Name this pair.

139. All-Star Game MVP honors went to the father in 1980 and the son in 1992.

140. Still a regular at the time of his retirement, this player was named World Series MVP while playing for the losing team.

141. Signing with Baltimore for the 1987 season, he became the first reigning World Series MVP to leave his previous club.

142. One of these men is not among the five original Hall of Fame inductees of 1936: Walter Johnson; Babe Ruth; Honus Wagner; Ty Cobb; Christy Mathewson; Cy Young. Can you identify the imposter?

143. These two receivers won the Rookie of the Year and the Gold Glove awards in the same season.

144. Which Hall of Fame umpire played outfield for the White Sox during the thirties?

145. He was elected to the Hall of Fame the year he retired.

146. Name the Commissioner who slapped the asterisk (since removed) on Roger Maris in 1961.

147. The Hall called for him in 1996, 104 years after he played his last game in the majors.

148. Teammates for the better part of their careers, Cooperstown made room for them both in 1974.

149. The Commissioner during the strikes of 1972 and 1981 served for fifteen years. Name him.

150. Honus Wagner was the first player to make the Hall of Fame as a shortstop, but the man who once managed against Wagner in the World Series was the next one.

151. In 1937 these three became the first men to be elected to the Hall as managers.

152. Name the only Texas Ranger to toss a pair of no-hitters.

153. This pitcher won his fifth and final Gold Glove at age forty-four in 1983.

154. The first two left-handed pitchers elected to the Hall made it in 1946, long after they died.

155. Identify the first double play combination to garner the Gold Glove Award in 1959.

156. Last alphabetically on the list of Hall of Famers, he died a year after his final season.

157. By the time this Dominican outfielder was twenty-five, he had already garnered five Gold Gloves. He would fail to win another at any other point in his career.

158. In 1964 Philadelphia had a shortstop who bagged the Gold Glove after having supplanted the Phillie who won the award the previous season. Name that shortstop and his predecessor.

159. Who was the first New York Met to win a Gold Glove?

160. He won his only Gold Glove in 1969 at the same position where his brother nailed his fifth and final honor six years earlier. Name them both.

161. This Rookie of the Year led the A.L. in triples in 1973 despite falling more than 100 plate appearances short of qualifying for the batting title.

162. After winning A.L. rookie honors in 1952, this player skidded into the doghouse the following season by dropping a big league high of 20 games.

163. Name the lefty who bagged the A.L. Rookie of the Year after failing to post a win after brief trials in each of his four previous seasons.

164. Despite the hoopla surrounding Atlanta's quartet of Maddux, Glavine, Smoltz, and Avery, it was this fifth starter who tossed a no-hitter in 1994.

165. This American Leaguer's .210 average in 1987 was the lowest ever for an outfielder who won a Gold Glove while also qualifying for the batting title.

166. He played shallow in center, but this National Leaguer's speed enabled him to snare eight consecutive Gold Gloves between 1975 and 1982.

167. In each of his last twelve seasons this Hall of Fame outfielder was awarded the Gold Glove.

168. Identify the hot cornerman who ended Mike Schmidt's streak of nine consecutive N.L. Gold Gloves in 1985 only to

have it snatched away by the Phillie third baseman the following year.

169. Willie Mays, Roberto Clemente, and this other fly chaser
bagged all the N.L. Gold Glove honors in the outfield
between 1963 and 1968.

170. After Vern Law won the Cy Young as a Pirate in 1960, thirty
years passed until Pittsburgh had a second Cy Young winner.
Name him.

171. In 1984 he became the first player to lead the majors in
homers and RBI who was not named his league's MVP.

172. This man performed the same feat as the player in the question above in consecutive seasons during the nineties.

173. He led the A.L. with 25 wins and 308 strikeouts but lost to
Vida Blue in the Cy Young balloting in 1971.

174. In 1996 this visiting hurler proved it is possible to toss a no-
hitter in Coors Field.

175. At 6'10" he stands as the tallest Cy Young recipient.

176. The first pitcher to win the Rookie of the Year Award started
and lost Game 1 and Game 4 of that year's World Series.

177. This former Rookie of the Year finished his career with the
Cards in 1988 after spending the previous season with the
Yakult Swallows in Japan.

178. His batting average during his Rookie of the Year winning
season proved to be 96 points below his career best.

179. Although this Magnolia, Alabama, native won Rookie of
the Year while with the White Sox, he actually debuted
with the Indians.

180. Six years after this switch-hitting shortstop won the A.L.
Rookie of the Year, he batted .195 as a regular for the same
club.

181. When Pete Rose was booted from the Red's skipper job,
this former Cincinnati Rookie of the Year served as interim
manager.

182. The first Yankee to win Rookie of the Year spent his entire career with the Bombers.

183. Name the man who won the most career games who also won an A.L. Rookie of the Year Award.

184. A Rookie of the Year at short, he later won an American League batting crown while patroling the outfield.

185. Despite wacking 40 doubles during the season he won Rookie of the Year, this third baseman drove in only 44 runs.

186. Ponce, Puerto Rico, cheered when this catcher and Rookie of the Year set a freshman record by stringing together a 34-game hitting streak in 1987.

187. While at second, this Rookie of the Year became the only National Leaguer in the twentieth century to walk 100 times.

188. One year before he won the A.L. Rookie of the Year Award, this free-swinger led the Pacific Coast League (AAA) in homers with 50 in 1982.

189. Elected to the Hall of Fame in 1987, he had won the Rookie of the Year Award twenty-six years earlier.

190. The first N.L. third baseman to win Rookie of the Year would later capture the A.L. MVP Award.

191. Not only did this pitcher win Rookie of the Year in 1952, he also started and defeated the Yanks in Game 1 of that year's World Series.

192. This former basketball star from the University of Oklahoma won 15 games during his Rookie of the Year season, despite not being called up to the majors until late May.

193. Who was the first Rookie of the Year to win the Cy Young with another team?

194. His 57 RBI in 1951 were 87 fewer than the total he amassed the previous season, when he won Rookie of the Year.

195. He hit more career homers than any Rookie of the Year winner.

196. Seven years after he pitched a no-hitter against the Mets in 1969, this hurler was killed in a car accident on his twenty-ninth birthday.

197. In 1974 this Cleveland hurler pitched a no-hitter, allowing only one base runner—a result of his own throwing error.

198. Six years after he pitched a no-hitter in the A.L., this player fashioned a perfect game in the N.L.

199. Identify the southpaw who was dealt to the Cards just one month after spinning a no-hitter for the Bucs in 1951.

200. Name the hurler who clinched his club's divisional title with a no-hitter in 1986.

201. This Red Sox lefty made the last putout of his own no-hitter in his final season in 1956.

202. Two years after playing centerfield for Cleveland during Bob Feller's no-hitter in 1946, this man fashioned his own gem.

203. This Venezuelan White Sox hurler pitched a no-hitter in 1991, just two years after becoming the first man born in the 1970s to play in the majors.

204. He was banned for life by Judge Landis three years after no-hitting the Browns in 1917.

205. Who was the first African American to be named N.L. Manager of the Year?

206. The Yankees let this MVP of the 1996 World Series walk during the off-season.

207. It should surprise no one that this man was named MVP of the 1956 Fall Classic.

208. A native of Los Angeles, this Dodger had the distinction of winning the 1959 World Series MVP as a rookie.

209. After spending eleven seasons with his original team, this player skipped town and won N.L. MVP honors in his first season with the Cubs.

210. Despite winning the Rookie of the Year Award as a starter, this man retired with over 600 relief appearances.

211. In 1983, because of the senior circuit's dominance, this Angels outfielder became the first American Leaguer to win the All-Star MVP in twelve years.

212. On May 17, 1956, the Cards dealt this outfielder to Pittsburgh even though he had won N.L. Rookie of the Year honors the previous season.

213. He was elected to the Hall of Fame in 1982, twenty-six years after winning the National League Rookie of the Year Award.

214. This skipper was the first to win the Manager of the Year Award twice.

215. Name the first Yankee pilot to be honored as Manager of the Year.

216. His second no-hitter for the Cards came in 1983, five years after the first.

217. Detroit saw him fire 2 no-hitters in 1952 while sporting a 5–19 record that season.

218. Name the first helmsman to win Manager of the Year while guiding a team who failed to win their division. They finished third in the N.L. East in 1987.

219. Minnesota's first no-hitter was spun by this lefty in 1962.

220. Toronto was victimized when this Cleveland hurler tossed a perfect game in 1981.

221. This Brooklyn Dodger pitched no-hitters in 1952 and 1956.

222. In 1971 this Cardinal picked up win number 200 and his only no-hitter.

223. He had already chalked up more than 280 victories when he pitched the first no-hitter of his career in 1960.

224. Tom Seaver threw his lone no-hitter while with this team in 1978.

225. In 1916 this Red Sox hurler named George no-hit the Yanks. The following season a Bomber pitcher, who was also named George, returned the favor at Fenway. Name this pair.

226. This two-time MVP sang his swan song for the Rockies in 1993.

227. His real first name was Arnold, but this outfielder who won the N.L. Rookie of the Year award with the Redbirds in 1974 was known by another monicker.

228. Name the man who won Rookie of the Year in 1957 by playing both the infield and outfield for the Yankees.

229. This reliever, who won the National League Rookie of the Year Award in 1986, saw his brother debut on the mound for San Diego in 1993.

230. The first man to play for both the Marlins and the Rockies won the A.L. Rookie of the Year Award at short in 1988.

231. After winning the N.L. Rookie of the Year Award in 1980, this pitcher was forced to miss the entire season five times at different points of his career.

232. Twenty-six homers flew off the bat of this slugger, who ended the L.A. Dodgers' Rookie of the Year winning streak at four in 1983.

233. Atlanta used this man a bit more at first than in the outfield when he won Rookie of the Year honors in 1990.

234. A native of Venezuela, this A.L. shortstop popped just 1 homer, and drove home only 33 runs when he won the Rookie of the Year Award in 1985.

235. This Toronto hurler came within one out of a no-hitter in his last two starts of 1988 before pitching one in 1990.

236. During the fifties, he set a record for third basemen by playing in 829 straight contests.

237. Name the Tiger pitcher who threw a no-hitter on his birthday on July 4, 1912.

238. Eddie Smith took the loss when this power pitcher no-hit the White Sox on opening day in 1940.

239. His second no-hitter of 1951 clinched a tie for the A.L. flag.

240. Eighteen years after tossing a no-hitter for the Red Sox, this man served as the umpire behind home plate for the two no-hitters spun in the junior circuit in 1923.

241. Nicknamed "Piano Mover" because of his off-season occupation, this White Sox hurler spun no-hitters in 1905 and 1908.

242. In 1953 he cajoled Browns' manager Marty Marion into giving him his first big league start, and then delivered with a no-hitter.

243. As a rookie in 1922, this White Sox hurler pitched a perfect game against a heavy-hitting Tiger lineup.

244. Prior to bagging 2 wins in the 1919 Series, this Red's moundsman no-hit the Cards on May 11 during that season.

245. The Dodgers claimed this Hall of Famer on waivers in August of 1915, just four months after he no-hit them as a member of the Giants.

246. He toiled for the Cleveland Buckeyes in the 1947 Negro League World Series and later spun a no-hitter for the Cubs in 1955.

247. During his Rookie of the Year season for the Braves in 1971, he slammed 33 into the seats, then saw his run production drop steadily until he finished with Oakland in 1977.

248. In 1984 the Hall of Fame welcomed this man who had won the A.L. Rookie of the Year Award twenty-eight years earlier.

249. His 35 homers as freshman receiver in 1993 made him a lock for the N.L. Rookie of the Year.

250. The last three Gold Gloves won by this A.L. outfielder between 1962 and 1964 were coupled with batting averages of .228, .225, and .208 respectively.

251. On August 19, 1969, this Cub lefty became the first National Leaguer to toss a no-hitter without recording a single strikeout.

252. While wearing Brooklyn garb, this former archenemy of Flatbush spun the last no-hitter at Ebbetts Field in 1956.

253. These two Orioles combined to no-hit Detroit in 1967, but lost the game 2–1.

254. Trumpbour was the middle name of this 1972 N.L. Rookie of the Year, who won 15 games while posting a 2.32 ERA.

255. The first A.L. reliever to win Rookie of the Year bagged 27 saves in 1989.

256. He was a major league catcher for twenty-four years, but won his only Gold Glove during his first full season.

257. He won over 300 games following his no-hitter with Buffalo in 1880.

258. Later the public address announcer for the Orioles, this man fashioned a no-hitter for Brooklyn in 1948.

259. This L.A. Dodger outfielder won the first of three consecutive Gold Gloves in 1971, eleven years after his debut.

260. Name the Angels' Gold Glove outfielder of 1978 who popped just one homer while driving in 37 runs.

261. The first Dominican-born Rookie of the Year won the honor while with the Dodgers in 1994.

262. After this Red Sox hurler was ejected for arguing with the home-plate umpire, Ernie Shore took the mound and retired 27 consecutive Washington batters in the first game of a doubleheader in 1917.

263. A rookie for Oakland in 1983, he tossed a no-hitter but was gone from the majors just two years later at age twenty-four with only 9 career wins.

264. Over 200 wins roared from the arm of this Hall of Famer after he no-hit the Red Sox in 1926.

265. The man who retired with the fewest career wins for any Gold Glove honoree garnered just 58 in a ten-year career spent entirely with Oakland.

266. He no-hit Kansas City and Detroit a month apart en route to his first 20-win season in 1973.

CHAPTER THREE
All-Time Leaders

1. Wildness, mediocre teams, and a long career helped earn him the distinction of having the most losses of any pitcher during the twentieth century.
2. Although nearly two-thirds of the games he played in his debut year were in the DH slot, this man went on to set a record for the most games played at first base.
3. A wizard if ever there was one, he set the pace with 621 putouts at short in 1980.
4. Mike Schmidt took the job of this hot cornerman who would set the A.L. record for highest fielding average in a season.
5. Breaking pitches were the bread and butter of this man, who set a twentieth-century record when he recorded 49 putouts while at the same time becoming the A.L.'s only 20-game winner in 1984.
6. Who in 1984 became the initial regular first baseman to field 1.000 in a season?

7. No outfielder has flagged down 500 putouts since this Oakland Athletic in 1980.

8. Only one backstop has fielded 1.000 in a season in which he caught at least 100 games. Yogi Berra didn't do it with the above criteria, but our man turned the trick the year Berra debuted.

9. When Chet Lemon set the A.L. standard with 512 outfield putouts in 1977, he eclipsed the mark of a fly chaser whose brother is in the Hall of Fame.

10. All but one of the top ten seasonal fielding averages among first baseman are held by men who posted their marks after World War II. The exception is this man who played behind Herb Pennock in 1921.

11. He set the record for putouts in a season by a first baseman but committed an infamous World Series fielding blunder the following year.

12. Possessor of a warm smile, the outfielder who holds the record for double plays in a season had the grin wiped off his face when Judge Landis gave him and his seven cronies the boot after the 1920 season.

13. No one had more assists at any position than this scrapper who threw for 641 at second in 1927.

14. The putout record for outfielders was set the following season by the above man's teammate.

15. Only one catcher has racked up 1,000 putouts in a season, and he did it twice during the sixties.

16. In 1907 he established standards for putouts and chances by a first sacker in a season, busting his own records set the previous year with a World Championship team.

17. More putouts were made in a season by this 1887 third baseman, who in that year also became the first hot cornerman to collect 200 hits.

18. He set a record, later tied, for putouts by a shortstop in a season while on the World Champs in 1914.

19. Gone after the 1930 season, this player shares the record with the man described in the previous question and is also the only shortstop to reach for 1,000 chances twice.

20. Fielding barehanded for most of his career with Cincinnati, this player outdistanced everyone at the keystone position with 529 putouts in 1886. His record still stands.

21. At third he set records for putouts and double plays in 1971.

22. In 1989 this player set a seasonal record, which was later broken, for highest fielding average at short. Five years later he posted the new standard in his first season at third.

23. Who is the only player to collect 3,000 hits while hitting fewer than 50 homers?

24. He wound up his twenty-three-year career in 1985 just one double shy of 500.

25. This Wahoo, Nebraska, native collected the most career total bases for any player who failed to hit 100 homers.

26. His hit total is higher than any other player who spent his entire career with the same team.

27. Triples rang off this man's bat more often than any other player whose career began after World War II.

28. This player, who last saw action the year Walter Johnson debuted, was the first to appear in 2,000 games at short.

29. Popularizer of the stretching one-handed catch at first and later a correspondent for *The New York Times*, he set an assist mark in 1905 that took more than three-quarters of a century to fall in the N.L.

30. A short right-field wall, a notoriously bad pitching staff, and a good arm helped this man throw out a twentieth-century record of 44 runners in 1930.

31. As a rookie he set the record for the most chances by a third baseman. However, the man who replaced him the following year holds the twentieth-century mark. Name these hot cornermen.

32. Upon posting the top two putout totals at first in 1949 and 1950, he proceeded to win batting crowns in each of his next two campaigns.

33. Noted for his comeback attempt in an independent league in 1996, this hurler holds the career record for putouts.

34. Name the outfielder who holds the career record for putouts.

35. Crouching behind the plate for nineteen years, he set the lifetime putout and chance mark for receivers.

36. Possessing great range and fleetness of foot, the shortstop who set the career assist standard once led his league in RBI on a John McGraw-led pennant-winning team.

37. This pitcher of twenty-four seasons who started the most double plays in a career won his last game at age forty-eight.

38. Proven to be one of the "clean Sox," he turned more double plays than any other catcher in a career.

39. The pitcher who holds the career assist record debuted in 1890 and leads the way by more than 500.

40. This National League second baseman of the 1970s set a record for most at-bats over a two-year period.

41. An abbreviated schedule didn't prevent this Rockie from establishing the seasonal mark for pinch hits in a season.

42. Eddie Murray topped the career mark for games played at first, a record previously held by a Hall of Famer who last saw action in 1907.

43. The man who shares a nickname with one of the most overpowering relievers in baseball retired with exactly 500 doubles and a .500 slugging average.

44. Notorious for coaxing walks, this man who never played a game in the minors was the first to play 2,000 contests at third.

45. Who threw 28 shutouts over two seasons during the teens?

46. He collected more extra-base hits than any man who played exclusively in the nineteenth century.

47. In 1995 Cooperstown called for the man who dropped a twentieth-century record 29 games in 1905.

48. This 300-game winner is the only man to start over 70 games in consecutive seasons.

49. No National Leaguer has rocketed at least 50 homers in a season since this man did it for a team coming off two World Championships.

50. Practitioner of a sidearm delivery throughout his career, this player won 109 games in a two-year span.

51. He went directly from the campus of Oklahoma State University to the big leagues and proceeded to fan 185 times as a rookie in 1986.

52. In 1970 this right-handed reliever became the first pitcher to appear in 90 games in one season.

53. His 254 hits in 1929 stands as the all-time N.L. high, but he drew his huge following for his Coast League achievements in San Francisco.

54. One of the game's most undisciplined swings belongs to the player who whiffed at least 175 times in three seasons.

55. Only one player drove in at least 150 runs in a season during the nineteenth century, and he did it twice with totals topping 160.

56. This receiver was deadly off the bench, rapping at least 20 pinch hits in 1965 and 1966 during the twilight of his career.

57. Dubbed "Cannonball," this fiery-tempered starter of the late nineteenth century was the first lefty to win 100 games. He still holds the single-season mark for shutouts by a southpaw.

58. Although not known for his power, this second baseman did slap an N.L. record 114 doubles between 1935 and 1936.

59. A $100,000 bonus was given to this highly touted slugger who most notably set the predivisional play record when he went down swinging 175 times in 1963.

60. This recordholder for the most losses in a season by a reliever officially ended Pete Rose's 44-game hitting streak the year before the pitcher earned his dubious distinction.

61. He retired one homer shy of 400 and two doubles short of 500.

62. This fierce competitor won the most World Series games of any pitcher who never played for a New York team.

63. Name the first pitcher to log 100 innings in World Series play.

64. Since divisional play this player won more World Series games than any other hurler.

65. These two hurlers appeared in 12 World Series games, the most for any pitcher prior to World War II.

66. The first man to collect at least 100 pinch hits also won over 150 games in his career.

67. Coincidentally, he died in 1961 after having driven in 1,961 runs.

68. Some of the finest pitching down the stretch was turned in by the only man to throw a complete game shutout in both a League Championship Series and a World Series during the same postseason.

69. During his career this lefty won 220 games, but in the LCS he was dreadful, losing all 7 of his starts.

70. A first ballot Hall of Famer, he issued more free passes than any other pitcher in LCS play.

71. It took a while for this hurler to develop, but once he did he set the LCS career record for wins and innings pitched.

72. This first baseman drove in a record 21 runs in LCS play.

73. Dangerous at the plate and deadly in the postseason, he popped more over the fence than any other batter in LCS history.

74. Provider of World Series thrills, this slugger holds career records for games played and at-bats in the LCS but only hit .227 in those contests.

75. Malaprops are the specialty of the man who played the most World Series games.

76. For years Pepper Martin stood alone with his .418 career average in World Series play. But when the 1993 series came to a close, Martin had to share the record with this man.

77. Fans saw him homer in the first All-Star game, but he never hit one in 197 at-bats in World Series competition.

78. His 22 RBI in World Series play during the thirties and forties are the most for anyone who never played in New York.

79. This wild man was the first hurler since 1900 to walk at least 200 batters twice.

80. Strong wrists helped him crank more World Series homers than any other man who did not wear a New York uniform.

81. It took this demon of the base paths only two Fall Classics to tie Eddie Collins's record for bags swiped in World Series play.

82. This native of St. Louis who pitched for his hometown team is the last man to log 100 starts over a two-year span.

83. Name the pair of clubbers who collected 100 extra-base hits on two occasions.

84. Opposing pitchers blew this star away 376 times over two seasons.

85. Two leadoff men have batted over 700 times in a season. The recordholder did it for a pennant winner in 1980, and the other did it as an N.L. freshman in 1984.

86. The last National Leaguer to amass at least 100 extra-base hits in a season is also the last player to slug .700 in a full season in the senior circuit.

87. This man was Puerto Rico's first native son to make it to the majors. He debuted in 1942 and went on to lead the N.L. in shutouts in 1943, but was shot to death on New Year's Day in 1952.

88. Who is the only player to club 500 homers while hitting fewer than 300 doubles?

89. Gone from the majors after playing one game with the Yanks in 1945, he is the only player who broke in since 1920 who also cracked the top ten in career triples.

90. Owner of 442 homers including 35 in his swan song season (a record for someone playing his final year), this man has not made the Hall even though he became eligible for inclusion in 1992.

91. In 1944 he became the first National Leaguer to amass 1,000 extra-base hits.

92. Although Hank Aaron bested Babe Ruth in career homers, he tied him in this major offensive category.

93. With over 1,000 thefts and still climbing through 1996, he has had three stints with his original team.

94. A key figure in back-to-back World Championships, this infielder stole a record 689 bases without ever leading his league.

95. He hit only 149 homers but fanned more often than either Mickey Mantle or Harmon Killebrew.

96. Name the player who had the highest career batting average among those who fanned at least 1,000 times.

97. This 500-homer man went down swinging only 709 times.

98. Name the first player to whack 500 homers and retire with a slugging average below .500.

99. While in Milwaukee's employ this man became the first reliever to net 300 saves.

100. He was the first fireman to top the 400 save mark.

101. Dennis Eckersley's 48 saves in 1990 fell 9 short of matching this stopper's major league record, also set that year.

102. Chuck Churn of the Dodgers handed this relief ace his only loss in 19 decisions in 1959.

103. A wad of chaw could always be seen tucked into his cheek as he won a record 99 games without ever making a start.

104. His combination of power and control makes him the only pitcher to fan 3,000 batters while allowing fewer than 1,000 walks.

105. The final save of his career in 1988 made him the first reliever to ring up 300 saves in one league.

106. Lou Gehrig was the second American Leaguer to play 2,000 games at first, a few years behind the man who did it that same decade.

107. He wound up with 2,488 games in the outfield, more than any other pasture patroller who played for only one team.

108. Selective at the plate, he walked over 1,600 times but batted under .250 in his career.

109. Lou Brock smashed the twentieth-century career record for stolen bases by a National Leaguer. The record was formerly held by a man who debuted fifty-one years before Brock.

110. Name the man who completed 92 percent of his 815 starts.

111. The antithesis of the man described above, this player failed to complete his starts 578 times but won over 300 games.

112. This second baseman's 1,865 walks leads all other infielders.

113. Born on New Year's Day in 1857, he fanned more batters than any other pitcher who played exclusively in the nineteenth century.

114. His 326 wins are the most among hurlers who never led their league in that category.

115. No one worked more innings and yet still failed to win 200 games than the man whose career spanned from 1951 to 1966.

116. A standout with Cleveland during the 1920s, this pitcher retired with 200 wins on the nose.

117. At one time he and Nolan Ryan took turns as the all-time strikeout king from start to start. Upon Ryan's retirement our man was more than 1,500 whiffs behind.

118. After winning 223 games toiling for a team who never won a pennant during his twenty years of service, he retired only to see his club win the World Series the following year.

119. The first player to appear in 3,000 games was hated by as many as those who worshiped him.

120. He tops the career list of shutouts by a lefty.

121. His 287 wins are the most by a hurler who was born outside the United States.

122. Logger of more innings than any other pitcher whose career began after the dawn of the lively ball era, he threw his final pitch at age forty-eight.

123. Of all the pitchers who broke in since World War II, he leads the way with 305 complete games.

124. He collected more pinch hits in his career than any other Hall of Fame player.

125. This two-time batting champ's .320 career pinch-hit average ranks him first among players with 150 or more at-bats.

126. One of the game's greats, this man retired with the highest lifetime slugging average among players who batted under .300 for their careers.

127. It may surprise you that the first man to save 200 games never led his league in that category.

128. He was the first player to collect 10,000 at-bats.

129. Ty Cobb's A.L. career at-bat record was broken by a man who played for only one team in his career.

130. Name the man who blasted a record 586 homers without ever hitting one inside the park.

131. The most productive right-handed power hitter of his time, he is the only man to pop 50 homers in a season for two different teams.

132. He hit more career doubles of any other player who failed to crack 50 in a season.

133. Totaling 240 safeties in 1985, he collected the most hits since 1930.

134. He cracked the top-ten list in career slugging and yet never led his league in homers.

135. This great rapped out 223 triples but never led his league in this offensive category.

136. He wound up with 3,574 strikeouts but never led his league in this category.

137. His .321 career average is the highest among players who debuted since 1920 and collected 2,000 hits without ever winning a batting title.

138. The lowest career batting average for any player with at least 300 homers who retired prior to the expansion era belongs to this Hall of Famer.

139. Gone after the 1992 season, he is the first pitcher to toss as many as 60 shutouts without winning 300 games.

140. Two natives of St. Paul, Minnesota, collected their 3,000th hit while playing for the Twin Cities. Name them.

141. Identify the first player to crack 500 homers who swung from the right side.

142. If you add up the individual doubles and triples totals of these two Hall of Famers, they both surpass the 1,000 mark.

143. He hit more career homers than any other lefty batter in N.L. history.

144. Truly a one-dimensional player, he swiped over 700 sacks yet popped fewer than 30 homers.

145. No man collected more career hits than this Hall of Famer, but he never picked up as many as 200 in one season.

146. This pitcher's career walk total exceeds the number of hits collected by Lou Gehrig.

147. His 242 triples are the most for a first sacker.

148. Name the Hall of Famer who lost more career games than any other lefty.

149. Among relievers who worked at least 500 innings, this man, who committed suicide in 1951, logged the highest winning percentage in history with a .708 mark.

150. He became the first N.L. player in the twentieth century to walk 150 times in 1996.

151. He is the only man to play exclusively in the expansion era who hit at least 400 homers, yet never fanned 100 times in any one season.

CHAPTER FOUR

Lifetime Major League Team Rosters

1. George and John Dovey were the presidents of which N.L. club that was once known as the Doves?
2. This Hall of Famer wore a Brooklyn uniform for more seasons than any other player.
3. The Providence Grays were represented in the N.L. from 1878 to 1885. Name the Triple Crown winner who was the only man to play for them in each season.
4. Which rival major league had teams known as the Infants, Wonders, and Burghers?
5. Willie Mays was not the only man to play for the New York Giants and the New York Mets. Can you name the other man?
6. A charter member of the A.L. and still going strong, this team was originally known as the Blues.
7. They joined the A.L. in 1902 and moved after the 1953 season.

8. Who is the only man to play for the Mets in the 1970s, 1980s, and 1990s?

9. For two years during the forties the Phillies attempted to change their nickname to one that was later adopted by an A.L. expansion team. What was their monicker?

10. What is the only team that has been continuously represented in its city in the N.L. since the league's inception in 1876?

11. Cleveland and Cincinnati have represented Ohio in the majors for nearly every season played since 1876. However, two other cities from the Buckeye state were big league entrants during the nineteenth century.

12. Which city once had a team called the Browns in the old Union Association?

13. This middle infielder was the last position player to play for the New York Yankees, New York Giants, and Brooklyn Dodgers.

14. One of the game's early relievers, he played for St. Louis teams representing the National League, American League, and Federal League.

15. He played on both the expansion Senators and Mets after having appeared for the Yankees in the World Series from 1949 to 1953.

16. A two-time 20-game winner, he is the only man to play for the Cleveland Spiders who lost a record 134 games in 1899 and then play for the Chicago Cubs who set the win standard of 116 in 1906.

17. This power hitter is the only man to play for the Braves in Boston, Milwaukee, and Atlanta.

18. Seattle saw this father of a major leaguer pitch for both Pilot and Mariner entrants.

19. Name the club that moved to its present city in 1968 after having shifted from its original location in 1955.

20. This New York A.L. team actually moved from a city that is currently represented by another junior loop entry. Name the city.

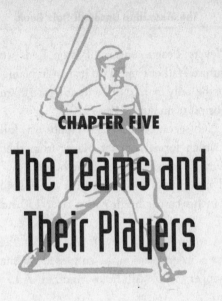

CHAPTER FIVE

The Teams and Their Players

1. Which Atlanta Brave is the only player to lead his league in hits despite missing as many as 20 games?
2. Who was the first Padre after Tony Gwynn to capture a batting crown?
3. In 1991 he hit a career high .327 in his seventeenth season, his only year with Milwaukee.
4. Injuries have kept this underrated hitter from attracting more attention. Playing for Cincinnati in the 1990s, he missed the batting crown one year by a point and finished in the top five contenders another year.
5. The guy who played the most games at short for the pennant-winning Pittsburgh team of 1902 was not "The Flying Dutchman." Can you name him?
6. The Baltimore Orioles' outfield of 1894 had the unique experience of playing in all of its team's regular season games. Name this trio.

7. The Players' League entrant Boston Reds won a flag with three future Hall of Famers on its roster. Name these greats.

8. Who is the only man to drive in at least 100 runs in a season for a Boston team during the 1920s?

9. When Cub second sacker Ken Hubbs was killed in a plane crash, which former cricket player from the Bahamas was shifted over from short to plug the hole?

10. He led the Orioles in ribbies with a lowly 46 in 1954, yet earlier in his career he drove in over 130 runs three years straight.

11. In 1993 when Ken Griffey, Jr., broke Seattle's club record for homers in one season, he surpassed the mark set by this free swinger, who still holds another A.L. club's season standard.

12. The only man to lose 20 games in a season for the Brewers also won 20 games for the Angels earlier in his career.

13. In 1993 they became the only team in this century to play an uninterrupted season without tossing a shutout.

14. Which shortstop played for only one team in his nineteen-year career but does not appear among the leaders in any of *The Baseball Encyclopedia*®'s yearly offensive categories?

15. Buffalo's entry in the Players' League featured this future Hall of Famer as its regular catcher.

16. Never a batting titlist, this player finished second to Nap Lajoie once and Honus Wagner twice.

17. A pennant-winning team of the 1980s featured a regular starter and an everyday position player, both of whom died during the 1990s. Name the team and its two players.

18. Which club has had the unique experience of having spent a season in the East, West, and Central divisions?

19. What was the first year both leagues played 162-game schedules?

20. Dante Bichette and the Rockies get knocked for producing big numbers in a hitter's park. What would today's media have said of this 1884 second baseman who hit all 25 of his round-trippers at home in a field where the dimensions were 180 feet to left field and 196 feet to right?

21. Steve Carlton won 27 games for Philadelphia in his remarkable 1972 season. Which teammate finished second on the club, a mere 20 wins behind?

22. Known for playing his heart out, this outfielder became the first man to lead his league in the categories of walks and at-bats in 1993.

23. Which team finished last despite having a 20-game winner, two men in their rotation who are in the Hall of Fame, and three outfielders who hit .325 or better, one of whom is in the Hall? To spice it up further, these players were managed by a trio of men who also made it to Cooperstown.

24. In 1940 this A.L. club boasted the first infield with at least 20 homers from each player. The team tied for fourth and were managed by one of the guys in this quartet. Name the team and the four players.

25. When was the last time two teams from the same city finished in last place in their respective leagues?

26. Which A.L. entry holds the junior loop record for the most losses by a first year expansion team?

27. This Oriole outfielder finished third in the 1971 batting race in the only season in which he had enough at-bats to qualify in his thirteen-year career.

28. This World Series championship team was the first club to feature an outfield where each man hit at least 30 homers. Identify the team and its trio of outfielders.

29. In 1963 they finished in third place, 13 games out, yet became the second team to perform the same feat as the team described above. Name this team and its players.

30. Since the formation of the N.L. in 1876, this "devilish" Louisville hurler is the only pitcher to work every inning of his team's regularly scheduled games in a season.

31. It was not "The Big Train" who was the first player to win 100 games with the Washington Senators. Name the man who holds the honor.

32. In 1906 they led their league in batting, runs scored, doubles, slugging, ERA, and fielding percentage but finished third behind a World Championship team that batted 49 points lower and scored nearly 100 fewer runs. Name both teams.

33. Reputedly one of the greatest fielders of his time, this first baseman was a league leader in errors in the N.L., A.L., and Federal League.

34. In 1936 these A.L. teammates combined to smack 115 doubles. Name the team and the two players.

35. Name the only player to hit over 25 homers in a season twice with the Kansas City A's.

36. Only one regular position player on the 1925 World Champion Pirates failed to bat .300. Name him.

37. Name the player who held Oakland's record for saves in a season prior to Dennis Eckersley.

38. Dubbed the "Blake Street Bombers," this Rockie quartet popped at least 30 homers each in 1995.

39. The last team to debut two players who went on to the Hall of Fame did so in 1948. Name the club and the pair of standouts.

40. Mystery shrouds the death of the first man to win a batting crown for a major league team located in Washington, D.C.

41. Toronto featured this trio who finished 1-2-3 in the A.L. batting race in 1993.

42. These brothers wound up 1-2 in the N.L. batting race of 1966.

43. Milwaukee featured the first Australian-born battery in 1993. Name them.

44. These teammates finished 1-2 in the A.L. batting race in consecutive seasons.

45. Which team was the last to score the most runs and allow the fewest runs in a season?

46. The Royals' leading winner in their inaugural season had shutout Walt Alston's troops in the World Series earlier that decade.

47. He pitched for Washington on three separate occasions during the 1940s and five times overall.

48. Name the only player who hit .300 for the expansion Senator outfit and had enough at-bats to qualify for the batting title.

49. The last pitcher to win 20 games for a big league team representing the city of Washington also led the A.L. in victories.

50. This third baseman was the last regular to bat .300 on the Philadelphia A's.

51. He was the first regular to hit .300 for both Houston and Montreal.

52. The first regular to hit .300 for an A.L. team in New York once won a batting title with an average over .400 in the nineteenth century.

53. A key member of the pitching staff of the 1927 Yankees, he was also earlier in his career the only St. Louis Brown hurler to lead the A.L. in strikeouts.

54. It was this George, not Sisler, who won the first A.L. batting crown by a member of the St. Louis Browns.

55. Name the Canadian-born hurler who became the first Texas Ranger to win 20 games in a season.

56. In 1996 Albert Belle broke the Tribe's all-time homer mark. It was previously held by a guy who hadn't suited up for Cleveland since the New Deal era.

57. Not only was he the first Minnesota Twin to secure a batting title, but he also bagged a second crown the following season.

58. When thinking of great Cub pitchers, Ferguson Jenkins and Three Finger Brown come to mind. However, this man holds the team's record for wins in a career.

59. The man who holds Brooklyn's career hit mark teamed with his brother Mack for parts of six seasons.

60. A publisher of poetry, this third baseman played the most career games in a Kansas City A's uniform.

61. Identify the Willie who holds the San Francisco Giants record for homers in a career.

62. While with the Boston Braves, Warren Spahn tied this spitballer's club record for career wins in the twentieth century.

63. This light-hitting infielder was the only man to play ten seasons with the expansion Senators.

64. In 1986 he played a club record 163 games without a miss for the Blue Jays but has recently grown accustomed to being on the disabled list.

65. Name the second baseman who was the first to play a season's full slate of games for the Atlanta Braves and the New York Mets.

66. Coming over from Kansas City, this man played in every game of the Marlins' inaugural season of 1993.

67. Despite 245 victories the only pitcher to have 20-win seasons with both the Cards and the Browns finished under .500.

68. His well-publicized, precocious debut helped him become the only pitcher to hang on with the Reds for fifteen years.

69. This receiver was the first man to play ten years in a Padre uniform.

70. Bidding to become the first team to play a 162-game schedule without getting shut out, they were whitewashed by Jerry Koosman on the final day of the 1979 season.

71. This was the only team to fail to have a single player reach 30 homers in any season during the 1980s.

72. Prior to Jose Rijo's capturing the N.L. strikeout crown in 1993, no Reds' hurler had done so since this man's whiplike motion intimidated the opposition in 1947.

73. They were the last of the original A.L. teams of 1901 to have a batting titlist. Identify the team and the player.

74. While managing Baltimore in 1901, John McGraw had the luxury of platooning a pair of future Hall of Famers behind the plate. Name the two players.

75. A former Negro Leaguer with the Philadelphia Stars, this player was the first to drive in at least 100 runs in one season with the Kansas City A's.

76. A charter member of the A.L., this team did not have a home-run champion until 1957. Name the team and its slugger.

77. As a result of the strike-shortened, split-season playoff arrangement, this club failed to make the playoffs in 1981 despite posting the highest cumulative winning percentage in the majors.

78. This Hall of Famer who played for Pittsburgh in the American Association, National League, and Players' League also died in that city in 1902.

79. Name the last A.L. pennant-winning team that did not have a single player on its roster with previous World Series experience. The team never won another pennant in that city.

80. In 1970 Washington had a reliever who was both fireman and arsonist, saving 27 games while posting a 2–14 record.

81. The 1987 Cardinals nabbed the pennant even though no pitcher on the staff won more than 11 games. Name the trio of Redbirds who tied for the team lead.

82. In 1990 he became the first Yankee to have at least 500 at-bats without hitting a homer. He also tied the record for fewest RBI by a player who appeared in at least 150 games.

83. This World Championship team set an N.L. record for the lowest batting average for a pennant winner, beating a club that won 109 games in the regular season.

84. Carl Yastrzemski led the A.L. in hitting during the pitching dominated 1968 season. Name the teammate who set the pace in RBI.

85. Detroit featured a trio of outfielders in 1925 who all hit at least .370. Name them.

86. A year before it switched locations, this team became the first N.L. outfit to sport six players who each cracked at least 20 homers. Name the team and its sluggers.

87. Back in 1894 this team set the record for most runs scored in a season when they played nearly 30 fewer games.

88. Although George Brett's name is synonymous with Royals' baseball, he finished nearly 200 hits behind the club's leader during the eighties. Name this batter.

89. Given an effeminate nickname, this player nevertheless set an N.L. record for wins by a lefty when he posted 42 with Detroit in 1886.

90. In 1986 he scooped up 36 saves for the "White Rat" to set a rookie record and would establish a new Dodger standard for number of saves ten years later.

91. In 1971 this Venezuelan shortstop drove in only 12 runs in 549 at-bats as a rookie for the Padres.

92. Four charter members of the A.L. in 1901 are currently represented in their original cities. Name them.

93. Identify the Federal League team that became the first club to win a pennant while nabbing fewer than 90 victories in a 154-game schedule.

94. The team with the highest winning percentage for a cellar dweller had won two straight pennants earlier in that same decade and would win another pennant two years after their basement showing.

The Teams and Their Players

95. This Connecticut-based club finished in third place despite posting a .691 percentage in the N.L.'s first season of 1876.

96. In its second season after shifting locations, this team won it all with a .564 percentage, the lowest for any team prior to divisional play.

97. While playing in a rival big league in 1884, this team posted the best winning percentage in history yet fell to last place after being admitted into the N.L. the following season.

98. Name the twentieth century pennant winner that played an uninterrupted season yet failed to gain 90 victories or have a single player drive in more than 67 runs.

99. He was the first man to play for the Kansas City Royals to make the Hall of Fame.

100. The first man who played for San Diego and the first player to wear an Oakland uniform and who were later enshrined in the Hall of Fame are one and the same man.

101. The pennant-winning Yankees of 1922 and 1923 featured a double play combination who appeared in all the team's scheduled games. Name this durable duo.

102. The Colorado Rockies had just one complete game pitched in 1995. Who turned in the route-going effort?

103. After being a bridesmaid in the N.L. batting race of 1971 and 1972, he won the crown in 1974.

104. Who finished second to Richie Ashburn in the batting race twice and to Stan Musial once during the fifties?

105. He hit 32 homers in his only season as a Yankee yet never played in the Bronx because of Yankee Stadium's renovation.

106. In 1993 he clubbed 20 homers, 10 for San Diego and 10 for Florida.

107. The first regular DH for the Texas Rangers was also the first player to collect 200 hits in one season for the California Angels.

108. In 1996 he became the first Met to garner 200 hits in a season.

109. Who cracked 25 homers for the Cubs in 1991 and 25 more for the White Sox the following year?

110. The last New York Giant 20-game winner was given a $65,000 bonus to sign with the Braves straight out of college.

111. Prior to Robin Roberts's 20-win season for the Whiz Kids, the last Phillie to bag 20 did it nine years before Roberts's birth and died the year Roberts ended the drought.

112. Who once won 20 games for the Mets and later spun a no-hitter for the Yankees?

113. They won 108 games and the World Series without having a single hurler win more than 15 games.

114. Their record-setting streak of having at least one 20-game winner for thirteen consecutive years was halted by the 1981 strike.

115. Shoulder and eye problems diminished the effectiveness of the last man to record 20 victories in a season for the Milwaukee Braves.

116. Breaking in as a reliever with Leo Durocher's Cubs, this man later became the first Milwaukee Brewer to bag 20 wins in a season.

117. Houston's first 20-game winner made his big league debut on his eighteenth birthday in 1964.

118. This bespectacled lefty was the first Royal to enter the 20-win circle.

119. These two San Francisco 20-game winners were not enough to stave off the Braves in 1993.

120. The 1927 Senators finished 25 games behind the Murderer's Row Yankees despite boasting a regular outfield trio who are now in the Hall of Fame. Name them.

121. Prior to Greg Maddux, this righty in 1974 was the last Atlanta Brave to win an ERA title.

122. Baltimore's first A.L. ERA champ was subsequently elected to the Hall of Fame, but his name is not Palmer. Can you identify this pitcher?

123. Even followers of the contemporary scene will have to pause before naming the first chucker to win the A.L. ERA title while pitching his home games in the hitter's haven Metrodome.

124. During his team's championship years from 1906 to 1908, this Cub led the N.L. in winning percentage each season, going 60–15 for an overall .800 mark.

125. Who led the Federal League in appearances in 1915 with St. Louis and repeated in this category the following year with St. Louis in the A.L.?

126. One of the nineteenth century's greatest stars was this lefty swinger who became the first batting titlist to represent Brooklyn. He later served as night watchman and press box attendant of the Polo Grounds.

127. In 1973 they became the last club to finish below .500 despite boasting two 20-game winners. Name the team and the pair of aces.

128. A year before winning their first pennant, they became the only team in this century to sport a pair of 20-game winners while finishing as low as sixth. Peg the team and the two starters.

129. Which Hall of Famer had at least one season where he batted over .300 with at least 500 at-bats for St. Louis in both the N.L. and A.L.?

130. The first Blue Jay to drive in at least 100 runs in one season was dealt to Cleveland in 1988 to make room for Fred McGriff.

131. In 1985 the Reds became the first team to have five players on its roster simultaneously who had each collected at least 2,000 hits in his career. Name this quintet.

132. Mike Stanley cracked three homers in the first game of a doubleheader in 1995 only to have Buck Showalter bench him for the entire second contest. Which Atlanta receiver also rode the pine following a trio of taters earlier that day in 1969?

133. Despite winning at least 100 games in both 1915 and 1961 this team finished second to the Red Sox and to the Yankees, respectively.

134. They won over 90 games between 1905 and 1908 yet failed to win a pennant during that time.

135. Name the only team to win at least 90 games in twelve straight seasons.

136. This precocious expansion team finished just 10 games out of first in their sophomore year.

137. When Reggie Jackson won home-run crowns in 1975, 1980, and 1982, he shared those titles with a different Brewer. Name each Milwaukee mauler.

138. Seattle's .300-hitting left fielder of 1986 was also Roger Clemens's twentieth strikeout victim on April 29, contributing to Clemens's setting of a new nine-inning record.

139. Ten years after the achievement mentioned above, the "Rocket" repeated his feat when he blew away this Detroit third baseman.

140. With the ascendancy of their righty-lefty duo in 1959 this team became the first to fan at least 1,000 batters.

141. Identify the first-year expansion team that became the second club to fan over 1,000 batters.

142. Bob Gibson shut out every team that opposed him in 1968 with the exception of this club that finished 21 games out while ironically scoring the fewest runs in the N.L.

143. In 1962 this team had the first double play combo who each fanned at least 100 times. Name the team and the dynamic duo.

144. Between 1977 and 1991 this lefty pitched for nine different teams, including two stints each with Montreal and Minnesota.

145. Minnesota had its first regular bat .300 in its initial season in the Twin Cities. Name him.

146. The last pitcher to start a game under Casey Stengel was this Met who finished the 1965 season at 1–10.

147. While at short for the 1945 Tigers, he became the only regular with over 400 at-bats on a pennant-winning team in the twentieth century to bat under .200. This man might have seen less playing time had he not been the manager's son-in-law.

148. A trio of Braves hit at least 40 homers each in 1973. Name this threesome.

149. Toronto had its first 20-game winner in this man.

150. Although Johnny Bench's name is synonomous with Cincinnati catching, this backstop set the team record for the most games caught in a season with 155 in 1944.

151. When the Phillies won the World Series in 1980, they carried this hurler, who finished with a dismal 4–14 record.

152. The first regular to bat .300 for the Orioles had previously played for the Memphis Red Sox in the Negro Leagues.

153. This utility player was the initial man drafted by the Blue Jays and its first regular to bat .300.

154. They finished only 1^1/2 games behind in their division in 1979 yet didn't have a single player crack more than 9 homers. Provide the team and the "slugger."

155. In 1973 St. Louis used three brothers in their outfield who hailed from Puerto Rico. Name them.

156. Because Uncle Sam snatched away their stars they became the first team to finish under .500 after having won at least 100 games the previous season.

157. Other than Cobb, the only other player whose given name was Tyrus reached his apex when he batted .314 as a regular outfielder on the 1921 Cubs.

158. After finishing in the basement with a .196 winning percentage in 1889, this American Association club turned it around and won their league's pennant the following year.

159. Montreal had its initial 20-game winner in this junior whose father pitched 7 games for the White Sox in 1951.

160. Between 1961 and 1976 this native of Detroit hit exactly 200 round-trippers for his hometown team.

161. When the Red Sox won the World Championship in 1918, who led the team in homers and ribbies?

162. He set an N.L. record when he fanned 153 batters in relief for the Phillies in 1970.

163. This Texas shortstop set a record in 1996 when he drove home 92 of his 99 runs while batting in the ninth slot.

164. Detroit's closer in 1970 saved 27 games yet retired with only 35 total saves to his credit.

165. The last pitcher from the original Senators to win an ERA title did it in 1928 as a starter and reliever. Name him.

166. Although the 1927 Yankees are remembered for their awesome offensive attack, they did feature the top three hurlers in ERA. Name this trio.

167. Name the team Eddie Mathews was with when he cracked his 500th homer in 1967.

168. They recorded their all-time lowest franchise winning percentage (.329) and finished 55 games out of first place in 1912.

169. Identify the first baseman who was the only player to win back-to-back batting crowns while wearing a Brooklyn uniform.

170. This Hall of Famer was the first Tiger to lead the A.L. in homers.

171. When Oakland won the A.L. West from 1971 to 1975, which pitcher garnered the most victories for them over that period?

172. He led the Yankees in the same category as the man described above during their World Championship years between 1949 and 1953.

173. The Tigers' first 20-game winner turned the trick in his rookie season in 1901 yet finished with only 39 total wins. He died at age thirty-six.

174. Cleveland's first 20-game winner in the A.L. had earlier posted seasons of at least 15 victories for the Phillies and the Athletics.

175. The Mets' first 20-game winner turned the trick five times in his career.

176. Babe Ruth displaced this man, who died at age ninety-one in 1986, as the Yankees' right fielder.

177. This bespectacled twirler won 20 games for the pennant-winning Pirates in 1927 and died on New Year's Day in 1990 at age ninety-four.

178. Toeing the rubber at 6'7", this native of Love, Mississippi, led the A.L in walks as a Yankee in 1918. More notably, he was the tallest player prior to the lively ball era.

179. In 1996 Mike Mussina became the second Oriole to fan at least 200 batters in a season. Who was the first?

180. He became the first Marlin to drive in at least 100 runs in 1995.

181. He stole at least 50 bases in a season for each of the following teams: Montreal, Atlanta, and Texas.

182. Seattle never had a player collect 200 hits until this twenty-one-year-old came along.

183. Tino Martinez drove in 117 runs the year he replaced this Yankee at first base.

184. When this Brewer was switched to the outfield in 1985, Ernest Riles took his job at short.

185. Dave Cash edged him out of his second-base job with the Bucs.

186. Paul Schaal was stationed at third for the Royals until this mainstay came along.

187. Prior to his debut, Lenn Sakata and Mark Belanger were platooned at short for the Orioles.

188. Clyde Barnhart was shifted from third to the outfield in order to make room for this Pirate star.

189. To fill the hole left by this Hall of Famer's retirement, the Cubbies shifted Bill Everitt from third to first in 1898.

190. Don Zimmer replaced this waning Hall of Famer at short in 1958.

191. Clete Boyer succeeded this Hall of Famer after his move to Houston in 1967.

192. Doug DeCinces spelled this spectacular fielding third baseman as a regular in 1976.

193. Roy Cullenbine took over the Tigers' first-base job after this clubber went to Pittsburgh.

194. Chuck Ward was the replacement for this pantheon player at short in 1917.

195. Charlie James lost his left-field post when this future 3,000-hit man came over from the Cubs in 1964.

196. Garry Maddox supplanted this great as the Giants regular center fielder.

197. Wally Pipp relinquished his first-base job to this Yankee Hall of Famer in 1925.

198. George Kelly was shifted to second so this future .400 hitter could play first in 1925.

199. The Red Sox used Billy Goodman and Ted Lepcio as stop gaps in 1951 after this Hall of Fame keystone sacker retired.

200. After this Tiger great's skills eroded, Jimmy Bloodworth stepped in at second in 1942.

201. Ed Bouchee took a hike when the Cubs shifted this Cooperstown inductee from short to first in 1962.

202. Chico Carrasquel gave this forty-three-year-old shortstop a rest when he took over for the White Sox in 1950.

203. Cito Gaston became expendable when this man stepped off the campus of the University of Minnesota in 1973 and into San Diego's starting right-field slot the next year.

204. Duane Josephson was among many who crouched behind the plate at Fenway in 1971 until this guy came along to provide stability the following season.

205. The only N.L. team to win at least 100 games for three straight seasons placed second to the Cubs in its fourth attempt.

206. Henry Cotto's hopes of remaining in center for Seattle were dashed when this teenager hit town.

207. Barry Foote's catching days were over in Montreal when this receiver snatched his job.

208. Bump Wills was given the boot when the Cubs moved this future mainstay from third base to second in 1983.

209. Glenn Davis was dealt when this first baseman joined Houston's scene in 1991.

210. Aaron Ward lost his second-base job with the Yankees in 1926 after this terror was called up from the Pacific Coast League.

211. Mike Hershberger was this slugger's predecessor in right field for the A's.

212. Don Lund's stay in right for Detroit was ended by this man in 1954.

213. Bruce Bochte's days at first were numbered when Oakland brought up this hulking clout master.

214. Don Blasingame's services at the keystone sack in Cincinnati were no longer needed when this great hit maker stepped up in 1963.

215. The first man to collect at least 200 hits in a season for the New York Giants was this outfielder who ended his big league career with 2,536 hits and a .316 lifetime average.

216. Although he was the first 200-hit man for the Texas Rangers, this third baseman failed to bat .300 that year.

217. Name the first Colorado Rockie to collect 200 hits in a season.

218. Receivers are generally slow afoot, but this former backstop led the N.L. in steals for 1994 while playing second base.

219. When Rickey Henderson stole a record 130 sacks in 1982, which Blue Jay second baseman finished a distant second with 54?

220. Maury Wills's speed dominated the N.L. to such a degree that his 104 swipes in 1962 more than tripled the efforts of this teammate and closest competitor.

221. This shortstop was the first A.L. player since Ty Cobb to snag 50 or more bases for five straight seasons.

222. After placing runner-up to Lou Brock in the N.L. stolen base race with 59 in 1974, this speedster proceeded to lead the senior circuit the next two years.

223. Identify the outfielder who led the A.L. with only 15 steals in 1950, 9 more than his Hall of Fame sibling had at any point in his career.

224. Nicknamed "Deerfoot," this outfielder and longtime roommate of Walter Johnson paced the A.L. in thefts in 1912 and 1913 with a combined total of 163.

225. Born Maximilian Carnarius, he led the N.L. in steals ten times during the 1910s and 1920s.

226. In 1953 Pittsburgh first laid eyes on these identical twins who served as a double play combo.

227. His second 50-homer season is even more impressive when one notices that his total represented more than half of his team's output.

228. A boating accident in Florida killed these two Cleveland relievers on March 23, 1993.

229. Tragedy struck the Tribe again during the 1993 off-season when this twenty-nine-year-old lefty was killed in a truck accident.

230. Which Hall of Fame teammate of Rogers Hornsby finished second to the "Rajah" in the N.L. batting races of 1923 and 1925?

231. John Leary must have felt like his name when the Browns began phasing him out in favor of this Hall of Fame first sacker in 1915.

232. Bernie Allen and Cesar Tovar shared second base for the Twins the year before this bat magician took over.

233. Brooklyn's last 200-hit man achieved the feat in 1949.

234. The last player on the original Senators to drive in 100 runs in a season did it in 1960.

235. His 19 homers and 70 ribbies outpaced all other Brownie batters during their final season in St. Louis in 1953.

236. No pitcher born outside the United States led the A.L. in strikeouts until this Cuban's three-year reign from 1961 to 1963.

237. Which post-1920 team won the World Championship yet failed to have a single player crack more than 12 homers?

238. Dazzy Vance's seven-year streak of N.L. strikeout titles was snapped in 1929 by this Cub who also took top honors in wins.

239. Which Hall of Famer was the last National Leaguer to lead the league in ERA prior to Sandy Koufax's five straight titles from 1962 to 1966?

240. This rookie led the N.L. with 56 stolen bases in 1995, but was traded after stealing only 8 bases the following year.

241. Walter Johnson saw his eight-year run as A.L. strikeout leader end when this Hall of Fame Tribe hurler finished first in that category in 1920.

242. Name the switch-hitter who became the first Padre to wallop 40 homers in a season in 1996.

243. Cleveland's single-season record for hits is 233. It was set by a man who was later given the boot by Commissioner Landis.

244. Wid Mathews was dealt to Washington so that this man could take his place in center for the Philadelphia A's in 1924.

245. Wally Clement and others were just keeping Brooklyn's left-field job warm for this native of Hamilton, Missouri, who stepped in as the regular in 1910.

246. Ripper Collins gave way to this Cardinal first baseman after platooning with him in 1936.

247. Dave Robertson lost his right-field job with the New York Giants when this Hall of Famer jumped in for the 1918 season.

248. Jack Fournier was no longer seen at first for the Cards after this Cooperstown inductee supplanted him in 1923.

249. In 1972 this Minnesota Twin led all shortstops in either league with a .276 average. Two months after the close of the 1976 campaign, he succumbed to leukemia at the age of twenty-nine.

250. He was the only A.L. ERA qualifier to record a mark below 3.00 during the heavy-hitting season of 1996.

251. Owner of over 2,000 hits and 1,200 RBI, this man filled in at left field for the Red Sox during Ted Williams's last two years of service in World War II.

252. As "Joltin' Joe's" replacement in 1944, this man posted a .300 average while knocking in 103 runs.

253. Brooklyn tried to move this Hall of Famer back to short when Pee Wee Reese answered Uncle Sam's call in 1943.

254. The Yankees reemployed this veteran at short to serve as their regular for a year before Phil Rizzuto's return from the service.

255. Mike Garbark, Rollie Hemsley, and Aaron Robinson all took turns crouching behind the bat when this fading Yankee star marched off to war.

256. Born Casimir Kwietniewski, he filled the White Sox's hole at short during Luke Appling's absence in 1945.

257. Al Bridwell replaced this Hall of Famer as the Cub's regular shortstop in 1913 after he was dealt away to become the Red's player-manager.

258. Ty Cobb led the A.L. in hits outright seven times during the deadball era. However, in 1919 his eighth and final leadership was shared with a teammate who also finished second to Cobb in that year's batting race.

259. When Rod Carew won the A.L. batting title in 1974, which fellow second sacker wound up second with a .316 figure?

260. As a result of the juiced ball of 1930, this Hall of Fame third baseman's .379 average only placed him fifth in the N.L. batting race.

261. This Brooklyn shortstop led the N.L. with 164 hits in 1919, the lowest total to lead the league in a season that was not interrupted by war or a strike.

262. Chosen first in the initial June free agent draft of 1965, this fly chaser led the A's with 14 homers and 58 RBI in the team's final season in Kansas City.

263. Bill Wilson's 15 homers in 1954 were enough to lead this team just prior to their relocation after staying in the same city for fifty-four seasons.

264. Playing his twentieth season in the bigs, this man clouted a career-high 19 homers, leading the Blue Jays in their maiden year.

265. Despite posting a .386 average, hitting 40 homers, and driving in 170 runs, this Phillie outfielder failed to lead the N.L. in any of the Triple Crown categories in 1930.

266. Babe Ruth was so dominant in 1920 that his 54 homers surpassed this Brownie sensation's runner-up total by 35.

267. Before the team's move to Texas the following year, this man closed out the expansion Senators' tenure in Washington by leading the A.L. with 22 losses.

268. Identify the outfielder dubbed "Downtown" who led all Padres regulars in batting during their inaugural season.

269. Texas had only one pitcher win as many as 10 games in the team's first season, and this guy's your man.

270. Between 1974 and 1987 Mike Schmidt led the Phillies in homers each year with the exception of 1977 and 1978. Which stocky slugger copped top honors both seasons?

271. Twenty-five homers was all this third baseman needed to lead the Colorado Rockies in their initial year.

CHAPTER SIX

Home/Road Performance

(INCLUDES WINNING AND LOSING STREAKS, DAYS IN FIRST PLACE, AND SEASON STARTING AND ENDING DATES)

1. Which team won the pennant despite an 11-game losing streak in 1951?

2. In 1949 this team, notorious for its dominance at home, played at a .792 clip at its local haunt but plunged to .455 on the road. Uncharacteristically, the team played twenty-eight percentage points better away from home when winning the division's flag in 1995.

3. Sure this club played .727 at home, but they also posted .800 on the road.

4. They were on the road to nowhere with a .429 mark. But their sizzling .767 at home was good enough to capture the 1902 A.L. pennant by 5 games.

5. Another flag winner who struggled on the road went .701 at Sportsman's Park and .455 everywhere else.

6. Name the year and the two teams that squared off in the last Fall Classic in which both clubs led their league in winning percentage both at home and on the road.

7. Despite the Tribe's dominance in 1995, another team in the A.L. Central spent fifteen days atop the pack only to finish 35 games out. Can you name them?

8. Although tied for five days, this World Championship team set a record for most days in first place.

9. Opposing pitchers were rattled when this team plated 625 runs at home in 1950.

10. Which club pounded out a record 133 dingers in their home park?

11. The team that broke the above club's record did it in a strike season. Once the park comes to mind, the team will quickly follow.

12. Before 1996, and not counting the strike season of 1994, when was the last year the regular season ended in September?

13. Prior to divisional play only one team pulled off a sweep in the World Series despite the fact that they didn't lead their league in winning percentage either at home or on the road. Name the team.

14. Both the team that marched into the Fall Classic after having been in first for only seven days during the regular season and the club that never saw postseason action despite leading the pack for 155 days were both managed by the same man. Name him and his two teams.

15. Even with a .722 winning percentage at home and a league leading .627 on the road, this team finished second to Stan the Man and the Cardinals in 1942.

16. Which N.L. team was swept in the World Series yet never lost more than three straight during the regular season?

17. This World Championship team played 79 percentage points better on the road in the first year in their new stadium.

18. Which pennant winner managed by Bill McKechnie had the unique experience of playing 143 points higher on the road than at home?

19. Two years after posting the highest road mark in the majors, they collapsed to 13–64 on foreign soil.

20. Even the Sultan of Swat couldn't save this 1935 team from the worst road record (13–65) in the twentieth century.

21. Seven years before its first World Championship, this team became the only N.L. club in the twentieth century to play below .300 at home and on the road.

22. They careened into last place with a 19–54 record on their own turf and then won the World Series three years later.

23. Only 6 homers were hit at this team's Crosley Field in 1924, the low since 1920.

24. This ballclub sat atop the N.L. for 127 days in 1934 and 130 days the following year yet failed to win the pennant in either season.

25. In 1933 this crew led their league with a .689 mark at home. Remarkably, this was a 116-point drop from their previous season.

26. These guys, who have since changed cities twice, played over .500 at home yet lost their way on the road, falling below .200 in 1945.

27. Off to a strong start in 1908, this team sank to the basement after spending thirty-eight days ahead of the pack.

28. It should come as no surprise that the team with the worst ERA of all-time surrendered a record 644 runs at home and 555 tallies on the road.

29. A 21-game losing streak to open the 1988 season sent this team deep into the cellar from the get-go.

30. Which first-year expansion club treated their fans to a 20-game losing streak?

31. In 1932 they became the first team to crack at least 100 round-trippers in their own park.

32. Excluding the strike of 1994, what year saw the regular season end on September 2, the earliest date ever?

33. The only N.L. team in the twentieth century to win no more than 2 consecutive games during the regular season featured a Hall of Famer who tied for the league lead in homers.

34. The last A.L. team to turn the same woeful trick finished 13 games behind perennial tail-ending Philadelphia in 1939.

35. Discounting strike years, name the only club since 1920 to score fewer than 200 runs at home. They averaged 2.5 runs per game in a ballpark they shared with a team who scored 151 more total runs and still finished last.

36. Since 1920 no team has surrendered fewer than 200 runs at home in a season that featured a full slate of games. These guys came the closest with 207 in 1958.

37. The longest winning streak in the Federal League (15 games) was set by a pennant winner whose city now represents Cincinnati's Triple A affiliate in the American Association.

38. Of the original A.L. entrants of 1901, which one had to wait the longest until they reeled off 10 straight victories in a season?

39. Which expansion team had a winning record at home in its first year?

40. This team failed to spend a single day in first place in each of the last six seasons prior to divisional play.

41. They finished fifth in the A.L. inaugural season of 1901 despite featuring the longest winning streak (11) in either major league.

42. Their 55 wins on the road in 1971 is an all-time record.

43. The last team to hit fewer than 10 homers in their own park during the regular season did it during the 1931 campaign.

44. This club became the first outfit to win 80 percent of its home games in the same year it captured its third straight A.L. pennant. Name the team and the year.

45. In 1902 this third place A.L. team had the singular experience of being the only junior circuit club to record a winning record in visiting territories.

46. Despite becoming the first team to win at least 50 games at home and on the road, they failed to win the 1915 A.L. pennant.

47. Playing .740 on the road in 1909, this N.L. entrant had the best winning percentage in the twentieth century for any team that failed to win a flag.

48. A fourth place finish was the best they could do despite an all-time record 26-game winning streak in 1916.

49. An 18-game losing streak did not cause this seventh-place team to finish below the Chisox in 1948.

50. The best home record for an also-ran in this century was turned in by this second place A.L. franchise in 1930 when it posted a .727 mark.

CHAPTER SEVEN

Managers

1. Known for his front-office acumen, what was the highest position Branch Rickey ever finished in the majors as a skipper?
2. Who is the only man to manage in each decade from the 1930s through the 1970s?
3. The only man to guide teams that lost 100 games in both leagues later managed back-to-back N.L. pennant winners.
4. He won 103 games as a rookie pilot only to finish in second place.
5. Earlier in his career he guided four N.L. pennant winners, including three teams in succession. In his final season he led the Red Sox to a last-place finish. He died the following year.
6. Who was at the helm of seventeen cellar dwellers?
7. Which Hall of Famer, tenth in career wins for a skipper, began his managerial career in the Federal League?
8. The man with the highest career winning percentage never played a game in the majors. Who was he?

9. This flag winner and former player had three brothers who also spent time in the bigs.

10. He never managed to finish higher than third place in any season during his twenty-one-year career.

11. A tenth place finish was all he could muster as a rookie pilot. He was later dubbed "The Miracle Man" when he guided another club to one of the biggest comebacks in history.

12. He won two World Championships and a pennant in his first three seasons as a skipper.

13. Not one of his teams advanced to the Fall Classic during his twenty-six years at the helm.

14. His .537 winning percentage with San Francisco and the Cubbies is the highest among managers in over 1,000 games who never finished first.

15. This shortstop who played in five Fall Classics holds the record for the most games won in his only year as a manager.

16. As a player he appeared in just one big league box score, but he later managed for twenty-three years.

17. Nicknamed "Gunner," he has the distinction of guiding the same team to a pennant in consecutive seasons in different leagues.

18. Although he was named William, no one called him that during his four-year stint as the Yankee skipper beginning in 1992.

19. The first man to guide a team that won at least 100 games in a season never played in the majors.

20. Thirteen years after winning his second straight flag, this man died while managing the Tigers.

21. After winning 20 games and a pennant in his first year as a skipper, this manager never copped another flag in the following nineteen seasons.

22. Which Hall of Famer is the last player-manager to win 20 games in a season?

23. The first man to guide the Orioles to a first-place finish played in nine Fall Classics.

24. The first man to pilot Cleveland in the A.L. is also the only man to manage the St. Louis Browns for 1,000 games.

25. The Pirates retired the number of this manager who watched his charges sink to a sub-.500 record during his five seasons of leadership.

26. Given another crack in 1996, he's won more games than any other man who began managing since the divisional alignment who never played in the majors.

27. A native of Cuba, he is the only man born outside of the United States to be given the reins of a first-year expansion team.

28. He served as both the original Senators' last skipper and the Twins' first manager.

29. Which former Yankee star managed a team that finished ahead of the Bombers during its dynasty period of the fifties?

30. The last man to manage two clubs in one league in a season later won three straight pennants with his new team.

31. His playing career consisted of 49 games and a .181 average, but he would go on to win two World Championships at the helm of his former club.

32. Who was the last player-manager to lead his league in homers?

33. He stepped aside when Sparky Anderson took over the Reds. He also served as the original Brewers' pilot.

34. Under his leadership the Phillies became the last National League team to win at least 100 games in consecutive seasons.

35. The last man to pilot a tenth place finisher for a full season had hit over 100 homers while representing that city. What is his name?

36. They are the only brothers in the twentieth century to manage at least one full season in the majors. Both were replaced within a month of each other during the following season.

37. The only man to manage in the eighties who also played in the thirties once served as Billy Herman's double play partner.

38. Who hit the most career homers for any man who managed in the majors?

39. Most have forgotten this N.L. infielder with Cleveland and St. Louis who acted as a player-manager throughout the 1890s.

40. Who is the only man to win a game in the Fall Classic as a pitcher and subsequently manage a World Championship team?

41. This dental school grad had plenty of cavities in his lineup. In three seasons of leadership his charges never rose above the cellar, losing over 100 games each year for a career winning percentage of .301.

42. Much like the man above, he was a big league skipper for three years during the formative seasons of an expansion club that lost over 100 games each campaign.

43. His .373 winning percentage as manager of the 1922 Phillies is almost 30 points higher than his 56–107 record on the mound.

44. Not only did he pilot both Louisville N.L. teams but he also guided Louisville's only pennant winner in the American Association.

45. In 1934 this Hall of Famer had the unique experience of replacing the man who guided his team during his rookie season fourteen years earlier. Name the Hall of Famer and the man he supplanted.

46. Nine years after managing a first-year expansion team, he guided another club in the same league to a first-place finish.

47. In his first three full seasons this manager led the Red Sox to more than 90 wins each year. However, in his last three seasons he lost over 90 games each year.

48. With nearly 1,500 games under his belt as an outfielder, this man put himself in relief four times as player-manager of the Phillies during the forties.

49. Who is the only man to collect at least 2,500 hits and manage 2,500 or more games?

50. He has the distinction of guiding his club to its three initial pennants during his first three seasons as a skipper.

51. Known as "Bald Billy," he is the only man to manage at least 1,000 games in the nineteenth-century major league rival American Association.

52. The only manager to suffer two 100-loss seasons with the original Senators was also Walter Johnson's first skipper in the bigs and a pennant winner four times with the Minneapolis minor league powerhouse in the American Association.

53. Who is the only man to collect over 2,000 hits and win over 1,000 games as a pilot without ever serving as a player-manager?

54. This former outfielder was the first man to guide a World Championship team that played its home games outside of the United States.

55. Less than two years after his first World Championship, this man was dead from a brain tumor.

56. He played for the Milwaukee Braves and went on to guide the Milwaukee Brewers.

57. Phillies' management gave him the heave-ho despite the fact that his charges were sitting atop the N.L. West after 86 games in 1983.

58. In 1995 he became the first French-born pilot to lead a major league club for an entire season.

59. Last seen guiding the Mariners in 1988, he is the only man to be at the helm of six different teams for a whole season.

60. Which Hall of Famer died while serving as an active manager?

61. Name the pennant-winning manager who had a player on his World Series roster who was eleven years his senior. Take a shot at the player, too.

62. Only one father and son have managed in the big leagues. Here's a clue: Pop hit over .400 twice.

63. This native of Canada was at the helm of the last American Association pennant winner and the last Washington entry in the N.L.

64. A backup catcher behind Johnny Bench while playing for Cincinnati, in 1992 he became the first former Mariner to manage Seattle.

65. Who was the only man to pilot teams during the player strikes of 1972, 1981, and 1994?

66. Much hoopla surrounded Frank Robinson's being named as the first African American manager. Name the second; he was a fine player as well.

67. A winner of over 2,000 games in the minors, his major league claim to fame was that he replaced Casey Stengel as manager of the Boston Braves in 1943.

68. He was both the last skipper of the Milwaukee Braves and the first helmsman of the Atlanta Braves.

69. He was the only man to have a midget on his squad.

70. Several men have managed their sons. Who was the only father to watch his kid hit at least .300 for him as a regular?

71. After leading a crew that beat the Yankees in the 1964 Series, he jumped ship and grabbed the Bombers' reins for 1965.

72. With no previous major or minor league managerial experience, this man was given the Angels' job in 1973 because of his three NCAA championships with Arizona State University.

73. While with San Diego in the late eighties, reliever Greg Booker played for this man who also happened to be his father-in-law.

74. The first man to manage at least twenty years in the majors since the formation of the N.L. also won two batting crowns during the same period.

75. He had the unusual task of managing two of his sons simultaneously in 1987.

76. Only one former pitcher has won four pennants as a skipper. Name him.

77. Who was the last retired hurler to lead his charges to a pennant?

78. Fired as player-manager early in the 1952 season, he took his last turn at bat for Charlie Dressen's Dodgers in that year's Series.

79. Following a season as a pennant-winning, nonplaying manager, he went back behind the mask with his crosstown rivals, playing for the skipper with whom he had previously starred.

80. Red Schoendienst preceded and succeeded this fine pennant-winning strategist.

81. Many hurlers were terrorized by his bat before he guided the first Texas Ranger team.

82. The Astros' skipper in the team's initial season was also Mickey Mantle's first manager in professional baseball.

83. This player-manager led the N.L. in victories while capturing the league's first pennant in 1876.

84. A former batting champ, he was the first Astros' pilot to lead them to a .500 record.

85. Who guided the Mariners to their first winning record?

86. He was dropped by the Browns after the 1910 season when his crew lost 107 games, the most losses under any twentieth-century pilot who managed only one season in the majors.

87. He is the last man to be at the reins of an A.L. club that won at least 100 games yet failed to finish first in the standings.

88. In 1902 one of the games rough-and-tumble greats became the first man to manage teams in both leagues in the same season.

89. The only man to lead the Brooklyn Dodgers to a last place finish was elected to the Hall of Fame in 1996.

90. Oakland lost 108 games when this former first baseman called the shots in 1978.

91. His managerial career was off to a rocky start when the 1928 Phillies dropped 109 decisions. However, he turned his career around when he guided another N.L. club to a pair of pennants in the forties.

92. Who directed teams in the League Championship Series in the sixties, seventies, and eighties?

93. At the conclusion of the 1996 season only one man had been at the helm of the same team for eleven full seasons.

94. Prior to Sparky Anderson, who was the last N.L. manager to win four pennants in a decade?

95. Twenty-two years after he went 8–11 on the mound for the Cards, this man led them to a World Championship.

96. He directed World Series teams that lost to the New York Yankees but defeated the L.A. Dodgers.

97. Name the man who managed both for and against the Cubs in the Fall Classic.

98. The pride of Sheffield, England, this nineteenth-century pioneer is the only man born outside the United States to win 1,000 games.

99. A colorful figure, he was the last manager to catch more than half his team's games in a season.

100. Do you recall the only manager to also serve as his team's designated hitter?

CHAPTER EIGHT
Players and Pitchers

1. Who hit the most career homers without ever leading his league?
2. The man who holds the record for the most career homers while playing with only one team batted .196 in his first season as a regular.
3. You have to go back to 1912 to find the only workhorse in this century to lead his league in starts and relief appearances in the same season.
4. Which two teammates played their record-breaking nineteenth and final season together in 1995?
5. The 1937 Browns finished dead last despite boasting an outfield in which each regular player hit at least .325. Name these Brownie batters.
6. Only one man fanned at least 250 batters in four straight seasons. Sounds like Nolan Ryan, but it isn't.
7. This 6'8" right-hander was the last man to blow away at least 300 batters in consecutive seasons.

8. Two players had at least one 100-RBI season in the sixties, seventies, and eighties. Name these two big run producers.

9. He hit over 25 homers each year between 1950 and 1952 but retired with less than 100 primarily because he didn't get his first taste of being a regular until his middle thirties.

10. The last slugger to crack at least 40 homers three years running played for a team that never finished closer than 23 games out during that period.

11. Who was the last reliever to fan at least 150 batters in a season?

12. This man, who broke in to the majors since the start of divisional play, never saw postseason action in an eighteen-year career that covered over 2,400 games. His dad, however, played in three games during the 1961 Series.

13. Several players have walked over 140 times and many others have fanned at least that often. Who is the only man to do both in the same season?

14. He connected for at least 20 homers in each of his first fourteen seasons, an all-time record.

15. After winning his first start, this Mariner dropped his last 16 decisions in 1980.

16. Who had to wait until his fourteenth full season to win a batting title?

17. Although he once led the A.L. in saves during the seventies, this righty kept a packed suitcase within arms reach during the eighties. The Cubs had him in 1983, the Phils in 1984, the Cards in 1985, and the Tigers in 1986. He finally called it quits with the Expos the following season.

18. The only twentieth-century player to have two seasons in which he drove in at least 90 runs but failed to homer led the A.L. in dingers in 1901.

19. This star of the 1930s is the only player to hit at least 40 doubles while driving in 150 or more runs in consecutive seasons.

20. When Jack Chesbro set a twentieth-century record of 41 victories, the only pitcher to beat him twice had bagged 3 victories in the first modern-day World Series.

21. After driving in and scoring over 100 runs in 1993, this player missed the following season because of a broken leg.

22. In 1915 the Federal League banned the emery ball, seriously hampering two of their star hurlers' effectiveness. Can you name this pair of pitchers, whose win totals dropped a combined 28 games?

23. Which Hall of Famer collected a record 215 hits for Cleveland in 1898 without smacking a homer?

24. The only man to strike out at least 200 batters for a first-year expansion team accomplished this for a club that finished 24 games ahead of the guys in the cellar. Name him.

25. Because of World War II only two men played 100 games in each season from 1940 to 1949. Can you name them?

26. Who was the first big leaguer to drive in at least 100 runs in a season for a team who played their home games outside the United States?

27. The first A.L. infielder to crack at least 20 into the seats during one season is also the only minor leaguer to reach 60 homers twice.

28. Since expansion, this Tribe outfielder became the first batting-title qualifier to hit at least .340 without homering in 1980.

29. This outfielder, who died several months prior to his one hundredth birthday, scored 100 runs a season playing for the A.L., N.L., Players' League, and American Association.

30. Since the league-raiding wars of 1901 and 1902, when players jumped contracts at will, who is the only man to win at least 10 games in a season for both the St. Louis Browns and Cardinals?

31. Who was the only man to win 20 games for a Philadelphia A's team that was not managed by Connie Mack?

32. Name the man who won over 100 games on the mound, had a season of over 100 ribbies as a second baseman, and guided an infamous pennant-winning team as a manager.

33. In 1925 he became the first National Leaguer to hit 20 or more taters while striking out fewer times than he homered. Few noticed this feat because his brother led the A.L. in homers and RBI in the same season. Name the N.L. player.

34. The first 20-game winner whose father played in the majors was this junior who went 20–9 for Detroit in 1971.

35. He never played a game after he turned thirty despite having two seasons during the sixties of 30 or more homers to his credit.

36. Although the sixties was a period where pitching dominated, he was the only hurler to win in the double figures each year.

37. At the age of nineteen, he hurled 5 shutouts while handing Tom Seaver his first big league loss.

38. Name the two shortstops, one in the twentieth century and one in the nineteenth century to bat at least .300 while driving home 100 or more runs in four consecutive seasons.

39. Which two players stroked 40 or more doubles in seven straight seasons?

40. The only man to appear in 100 games in a season at all four infield positions played his fourth position while on the 1972 Reds.

41. Despite winning over 250 games, this pitcher retired with more walks than strikeouts.

42. Several hurlers have won 20 games in one year only to lose that many the following season. Who was the only man to do it in the Federal League?

43. Later an N.L. leader in wins three times, he played over 100 games at third base for the Phillies in 1934.

44. Which Hall of Fame hurler had a twelve-year gap between major league pitching appearances?

45. The first infielder in the twentieth century to fan 100 times in a season also scored over 100 runs for a team that finished last in runs in the junior circuit in 1934.

46. Name the outfielder who posted 37 homers and 138 RBI while playing for two teams in 1930.

47. Epilepsy, alcoholism, and partial deafness did not prevent this man from becoming the first to pitch at least twenty seasons in the N.L.

48. Only one man hit as many as 40 homers in a season while accumulating fewer than 400 at-bats. Name the player and the year.

49. Desperate for pitching in 1995, the White Sox briefly put him in their rotation even though he had not started regularly since 1983.

50. Although offense soared during the twenties and thirties, this shortstop, who quit baseball for pro football, was the only man during this period to bat under .200 with at least 500 at-bats.

51. He hit 25 homers for the Athletics in 1937 yet never reached double figures at any other point in his seventeen-year career.

52. It was either hit or sit for this lefty batter. Four times during the eighties he cracked over 20 homers without qualifying for the batting title.

53. Philadelphia's Ed Daily handed this N.L. win leader his only loss when he bagged a record 15 victories in one month in 1885.

54. In 1977 he became the first pitcher to win an All-Star game, Championship Series game, and a Fall Classic contest in one season.

55. Two men have won back-to-back home-run crowns only to miss the following season. Name these swatters.

56. Name the pair of 300-game winners who fanned at least 200 batters in a season with three different teams in the twentieth century.

57. Who won the most career games for any man who never qualified for the ERA title?

58. The last man to bow out as a 20-game loser won over 300 games in the minors. Name the pitcher dubbed "Kewpie Doll" and the year he lost 20 games?

59. Active in 1996, it had been twenty years since he last fanned 200 batters in a season.

60. He came in second for the 1982 A.L. ERA title despite never having started a single game that year.

61. Last seen with the Cubs in 1994, he is the only player since World War II to retire with at least 100 more triples than homers.

62. Marlins' fans were the last to see the only pitcher to appear in at least 400 games each as a starter and as a reliever.

63. After driving in over 100 runs for Brooklyn in 1945, this Puerto Rican outfielder jumped to the Mexican League.

64. Although he didn't throw his first big league pitch until after his thirtieth birthday, this man went on to pile up over 150 wins during the thirties and forties.

65. In a career that began in 1975, he became the first speedster in this century to swipe 20 bases for six different teams.

66. Boozing and brawling curtailed this flamethrower's career, and as a result he retired with the fewest wins for any hurler who piled up 2,000 strikeouts.

67. They were the first father and son to each fan at least 100 times in a season.

68. In 1885 the city of St. Louis watched as this second baseman's batting average plunged a whopping 142 points from the previous year.

69. Cub fans cheered this player who cracked the most homers between 1943 and 1945, when rosters were depleted because of the war.

70. Who led the N.L. in losses as a starter with Cincinnati in 1984 and then topped the A.L. in saves with Texas five years later?

71. After he fanned over 100 times without hitting a homer in 1991, the Blue Jays shifted him to short to make room for Roberto Alomar.

72. Name the two relievers who saved at least 40 games in a season in both leagues.

73. This shortstop led the A.L. in hits in 1968 yet batted only .276.

74. A future justice of the peace, this player won his sixth and final home-run crown despite missing 64 games in 1919.

75. The only man to play at least 100 games while averaging more than 1 RBI per game in his final season had his career halted by paralysis after the 1890 campaign.

76. He won over 15 games in a season with four different clubs and 14 for another during the 1970s.

77. In a career that began with the Phils in 1964 and ended with the Padres in 1982, he became the first man to win an All-Star game, a Championship Series game, and a World Series game.

78. A true workhorse, this bony right-hander appeared in a league-leading 90 games at the age of forty in 1987.

79. Nicknamed the "Terminator," he took a curtain call voluntarily after saving 36 games in 1995.

80. Who pitched in relief in at least 30 games in one season for nine teams?

81. In 1970 this center fielder posted the lowest slugging average of any player who had 200 hits in a season.

82. Only one hurler in the twentieth century started at least 40 games for five years running. If you think he pitched in your grandfather's day look out for a surprise.

83. He can lay claim to being the only A.L. switch-hitter to collect 200 or more hits in consecutive seasons.

84. Brushback pitches were second nature to this 300-game winner who posted ERAs over 5 twice in seasons in which he qualified for the ERA title.

85. This slick fielding N.Y. Giant of the nineteenth century was the first National League shortstop to lead the league in RBI.

86. The first shortstop to lead his league in homers rang up 12 "long" shots in 1900.

87. Which player who broke in with the Federal League went on to win over 150 games in the A.L., including one in a World Series start?

88. First among N.L. southpaws to win 200 games, you won't find a plaque for him in Cooperstown.

89. His real name was Arthur but everyone who saw this player, the only N.L. third baseman to drive in 100 runs three straight years, called him Pinky.

90. Vastly underrated, he was the only player to drive in at least 1,000 runs in the dead ball era who is not yet in the Hall of Fame.

91. Controversy tends to follow the only man to whack 50 homers and 50 doubles in one season.

92. Who is the only slugger to pop at least 50 four-baggers in a season without having played in the majors the previous year?

93. A line drive wrecked the career of the last man to win 100 games over a four-year period.

94. In 1898 this left-handed thrower became the first man to catch 1,000 games.

95. These brothers and teammates produced 460 hits between them in one season.

96. Two men collected 100 hits in the abbreviated strike seasons of 1981 and 1994. Name them.

97. For eighteen consecutive seasons he led the same club in four-baggers.

98. Highly touted in the late eighties, this starter won an ERA title while garnering only 5 wins.

99. The most recent player to collect 1,000 hits over a five-year period had his career cut short by glaucoma.

100. Starting in 1966, he qualified for the ERA title in each of his first twenty-two seasons in the bigs.

101. This Philadelphia A's first baseman was the only player to collect 100 hits in each of the American League's first ten seasons.

102. A live fastball helped this man become the only reliever to save 200 games before he turned thirty. However, he never saved another game thereafter.

103. It comes as no surprise that Pete Rose and Mickey Mantle hold the Reds' and Yankees' records respectively for safeties in a season by a switch-hitter. But it might interest you that both teams' former recordholder was the same man.

104. Homers flew regularly off the bat of this man in the minors. This first baseman and son of a major leaguer is the only swatter to bag 20 or more doubles and homers in his final season (1949).

105. An overpowering arm belonged to the man who won 20 games in the thirties, forties, and fifties.

106. Broad chested and possessing a potent swing, he was the youngest player to hit 500 homers, reaching the plateau at age thirty-two in 1940.

107. In 1996 he became the first man to drive in 100 runs while playing in both leagues in one season.

108. Head-first slides and aggressive all-around play were the hallmarks of the only National Leaguer to complete a season's schedule of games ten times.

109. His first 200-hit season came in 1982. The next time he reached that mark was a record nine years later. Interestingly, he did it a third time two years after that, and again in 1996.

110. Who collected over 2,500 singles yet failed to amass 3,000 hits?

111. A five-time all-star, he collected over 2,000 hits yet retired with only 15 dingers.

112. The N.L. lefty who won the most games prior to Warren Spahn, he spun over 300 innings while fanning less than 100 batters from 1921 to 1923.

113. While pitching for a first-year expansion team he became the last rookie to lose 20 games in a season.

114. Who was the last man to collect 200 hits while fanning less than ten times in a season?

115. Strikeouts were the specialty of the last man to amass one thousand innings over a two-year period.

116. What A.L. outfielder who played from 1975 to 1985 was known as "Disco Danny"?

117. The same season he hit 4 homers in one game this outfielder became the first player to fan 100 times in fewer than 400 at-bats.

118. Prior to expansion, no player fanned 140 times in a single season, but three batters went down swinging on at least 130 occasions each. Who were they?

119. Beginning with the Dodgers in 1958 and ending with California in 1978, this player drove in over 1,000 runs yet never drove in more than 77 runs in any one season.

120. The last man to drive in 150 or more runs in two straight seasons failed to lead his league in RBI in either year.

121. This first sacker was the first player in this century to pound more than 15 homers twice.

122. Born on January 27, 1896, he was the first man to live to 100 who played at least ten seasons in the majors. He also has the worst winning percentage among pitchers with at least 200 decisions.

123. The record for the most RBI by a player in his first ten seasons is held by a man who played for only three more years.

124. Despite fanning 382 in 1965, Sandy Koufax's total fell 131 short of this Baltimore lefty's total in 1886.

125. During the sixties this Hall of Famer collected 200 hits while fanning at least 100 times on three occasions.

126. Who was the first designated hitter to win a batting crown?

127. What pitcher led the A.L. in strikeouts in each of his first seven seasons?

128. Blacklisted from the Pacific Coast League because of a gambling scandal, he was the first pitcher to have a season when he led his league in strikeouts and walks in the twentieth century.

129. Name the man who hit over 45 homers one year and yet retired with fewer than 200 homers for his career.

130. Nicknamed "Camera Eye," he had five seasons where he collected at least 100 safeties, yet his walks exceeded his hit totals.

131. This Panamanian was the first American Leaguer born outside the United States to knock at least 40 over the fence in a single season.

132. One eligible pitcher who worked over 3,000 innings and retired with an earned run average under 2.50 is not in the Hall of Fame. He also beat "Three-Finger" Brown in the final game of a World Series.

133. Playing under an assumed name in his rookie year in 1918, this man went on to win more games than any other hurler who never won 20 games or fanned 100 batters in a single season.

134. Who was the only player to collect at least 100 hits in each of the National League's first two seasons?

135. Name the only player to drive home at least 150 runs while garnering 150 or more walks in one season.

136. This Texan is the only player to poke at least 50 doubles while swiping at least 50 bases in the same season.

137. In 1918 this infielder had the unique experience of being a teammate of both Ty Cobb and Babe Ruth.

138. Considered washed up by the Cardinals, he began his rebirth by winning a batting title with a first-year expansion team.

139. A native of Mexico, this man won a batting crown in the Mexican League and at the major league level.

140. His career hit total exceeds any other man who never played in the minors.

141. Which Hall of Famer had already pitched in both leagues while still in his teens?

142. In each of his first three seasons, this A.L. outfielder batted over .330 yet never again hit that high in his thirteen-year career.

143. As a result of war-depleted rosters, only one batter hit over 15 homers both in 1945 and 1946. Name him.

144. He is the only man to toss 30 shutouts in both leagues.

145. This Hall of Famer played under the name Eddie Sullivan as a rookie in 1906.

146. A former coal miner from Pennsylvania, he was the first switch-hitter to pound at least 30 homers while collecting 200 hits in a season.

147. Five years after the Giants debuted the first Japanese-born player, this former Cubs and Orioles fly chaser became the first former major leaguer to die in Japan.

148. When Mickey Mantle cracked his 111th career homer in 1955 whose A.L. record did he break for switch-hitters?

149. Who was the first A.L. player to win 20 games in consecutive seasons while pitching for a different junior circuit club in each campaign?

150. This A.L. slugger was the first to clout homers in All-Star, Championship Series, and World Series competition.

151. Not until his sixteenth season in 1985 did this man crack 30 homers in one campaign.

152. Two speedsters have led their leagues in steals while playing on first-year expansion teams. Name them.

153. Name the first catcher to drive in 100 runs in four consecutive seasons.

154. This man who served as a regular backstop batted over .300 for three straight seasons starting in 1991.

155. He played for a record eight different A.L. teams in a career that stretched from 1971 to 1988.

156. A minor league colossus, this outfielder closed out his big league career by leading the N.L. in whiffs while playing with Cincinnati in 1931.

157. This Brownie was the first player to pump 30 homers in a season in which he had more clouts than strikeouts.

158. He cracked exactly 24 homers every season from 1961 to 1964.

159. Déjà vu struck again when this outfielder poked 23 each year from 1983 to 1987.

160. Name the hurler who completed 15 starts, weaving 11 shutouts in one season. He also won the Cy Young Award that year.

161. Surprisingly, this guy drove in more career runs than any other player who never led his league.

162. The last man to spin 10 shutouts in one season dropped 7 of his first 8 decisions that year for the Cardinals.

163. He is the only man to win 20 games in a season for both the Philadelphia A's and the Phillies.

164. This guy turned the trick described above with the Cubs and the White Sox.

165. Carlton Fisk was nicknamed "Pudge." Another talented receiver who goes by that moniker was born the year Fisk popped his first big-league homer.

166. The last player to bat against Nolan Ryan is the cousin of a skipper who has guided a World Championship team. Name the player and the pilot.

167. This St. Louis Browns outfielder's 430 hits between 1936 and 1937 accounted for more than half of his career totals.

168. In addition to Nolan Ryan, only one other pitcher toiled in the 1960s, 1970s, 1980s, and 1990s. Name him.

169. A tough-hitting pitcher, he socked homers in both leagues during his ninth and final season in 1945.

170. He caught more of Walter Johnson's shutouts than any other backstop.

171. Upon jumping to the Mexican League after the 1945 season, this Cuban-born New York Giant infielder led that league in hits.

172. Who broke in during George Sisler's last season and played his final campaign the year Whitey Ford debuted?

173. In 1995 he became the first former overall number-one pick of the June free-agent draft to hit 300 homers.

174. This Hall of Famer bats leadoff alphabetically in the list of men who have played in the majors.

175. Between 1956 and 1966 this outfielder hit 131 homers, the most for a player who never qualified for a batting title.

176. Between 1980 and 1991 Rickey Henderson bagged the stolen-base crown every year but one. Name the Mariner who won the 1987 title.

177. One of the greatest hitters at his position, he batted .220 in 1941, a full 100 points below his career average.

178. Stuck on awful teams throughout his career, he is the only pitcher to win 20 games for a club that lost 100.

179. The last National League player to knock in 100 or more runs while hitting fewer than 10 homers did it for the pennant-winning club of 1985.

180. Switched from third base to the outfield upon his arrival with the Orioles, he scored exactly 99 runs in each of their pennant-winning seasons from 1969 to 1971.

181. Sparkling defensively and solid at the plate, this shortstop in 1893 became the first man to drive in 100 runs while playing for two teams that season.

182. This seventeen-year veteran first baseman was born the day Babe Ruth died.

183. Less well known is the infielder who batted .251 in 120 games for the Senators in 1966 and made his debut on this planet the day Lou Gehrig passed away.

184. He stole 31 bases in his career, but this former track star never played the field nor came to the plate in any of his 105 big league appearances.

185. Many have forgotten he teamed with the man described above, snatching 31 bases in 1976 while collecting only one at-bat.

186. With 22 wins for Baltimore in the American Association in 1888 and 28 more as Louisville's ace in 1898, he is the only pitcher to have a ten-year gap between 20-win seasons.

187. A former 18-game winner with the Cubs, this chucker has had three stints with the Braves during the 1990s.

188. Thirteen years after winning the 1945 A.L. batting crown, he was killed in a train accident.

189. He won the N.L. ERA crown in 1945 even though he had recorded 18 starts earlier that year in the A.L.

190. Once a 20-game winner, he pitched in both leagues each season between 1955 and 1958.

191. Banned for life, his .356 career average is the highest among regulars who are not in the Hall of Fame.

192. This Cardinal shortstop was the first player to collect 100 hits from both sides of the plate in one season in 1979.

193. Andy and Alan Benes teamed up for the Cards for the first time in 1996, but they have a long way to go to match these siblings' 49 wins for the 1934 Redbirds.

194. A teammate of the Benes boys, he added enough wins in 1996 to establish a new combined career mark among fathers and sons. Name the son and his father.

195. In 1995 the third brother in this pitching trio won 10 games as a rookie with Montreal. Name him and his two brothers.

196. This Kansas City A's hurler saw his two brothers debut during his final season in 1955. Name this trio.

197. Name the Yankee who set a record when he hit 6 grand slams in 1987.

198. The most recent man to lose at least 20 games a season in consecutive years had previously started World Series games for Brooklyn and Los Angeles.

199. Ralph Kiner saw his seven-year reign as the N.L. home-run king come to an end when this man won the crown in 1953.

200. Sandy Koufax won five straight ERA titles during the sixties. Which American Leaguer was the only other pitcher to win it more than once during that decade?

201. Supply the family name of the brothers Bob, Eddie, and Ted who were active in 1963.

202. While with the Cubs this infielder became the only batter since 1920 to have consecutive seasons when he failed to homer in over 600 at-bats.

203. The 268 innings he logged with the Tigers in 1961 represent the most of any opposing pitcher who did not surrender a homer to Roger Maris during his record-breaking season.

204. He stole 36 bases as a receiver for Kansas City in 1982 to set anall-time record, and later managed his former club.

205. Known for his unorthodox batting stance, he cracked all but one of his 301 dingers in the A.L.

206. This nineteenth-century star won his second consecutive batting crown despite dropping 100 points from his average of the previous year.

207. A true middle-inning and mop-up man, he appeared in 698 games in relief in his seventeen-year career, which ended in 1994, yet saved only 49.

208. Impatient and gruff, he is the only player to whack at least 40 homers and bat .400 in the same season.

209. Although he led his league in homers on four occasions, he had five other seasons in which he hit at least 40 but failed to win the home run crown.

210. Back problems curtailed the career of the man who hit at least 40 homers in three straight seasons but failed to amass 300.

211. Born and died in Georgia, he is the only player to smack at least 50 homers in a season while fanning fewer times than he connected.

212. He won batting crowns in the 1970s, 1980s, and 1990s.

213. Not only did he have 40-homer seasons in both leagues, but they came a record twelve years apart.

214. In 1991 he caught a record 88 games as a teenager with Texas.

215. Name the long-service hurler who led or shared his league's lead in shutouts in the sixties and the eighties.

216. As the result of an injunction that prevented this Philadelphia A's batting king from playing in Pennsylvania, this player was transfered to Cleveland where he became the first to win batting crowns for two A.L. teams.

217. His league-leading 23 triples with Cleveland in 1949 was more than twice the number of times this outfielder struck out.

218. The only man to collect 20 triples and 50 doubles in the same season did it for an N.L. team in 1946.

219. This first baseman is the only player to hit 60 doubles and 20 homers in the same campaign.

220. Dubbed "El Presidente," this first major leaguer from Nicaragua has won at least 100 games apiece in both leagues.

221. Since expansion he is the only pitcher to win 20 games at least eight times.

222. Only one man has led his league in starts for six seasons, and he did it consecutively during the fifties.

223. Huge and blazing fast, he set the record for whiffs by a reliever with 181.

224. Even though he never led his league in ribbies, this third baseman drove home more runs than any other player throughout the forties.

225. He swiped at least 50 bases each season for a record twelve consecutive seasons.

226. The first N.L. switch-hitter to pop 200 homers was a shadow of his former self after the 1991 season.

227. Name the only N.L. player to slam 100 homers over a two-year period.

228. This pitcher was the first number-one pick in the June free-agent draft to win at least 150 games.

229. After toiling on the mound for a record twenty-seven seasons, he called it quits after 1993.

230. This third baseman is the only American Leaguer to collect 200 hits in seven consecutive seasons.

231. As a rookie in 1927, he set a twentieth-century mark with 198 singles, while finishing second in his league to his brother and teammate in hits.

232. Since Ted Williams's effort in 1941, only one player has had a season where he had as many as 100 at-bats while batting

.400. Name this man who sparked an N.L. pennant winner down the stretch.

233. Never a 200-hit man, this Hall of Famer, who starred during the fifties, did reach 199 twice and 198 on a third occasion.

234. One of the game's most admired players set a record when he failed to hit a triple in 646 at-bats in 1989.

235. This chunky 200-game winner from Mishawaka, Indiana, had seasons during his career when he won 14, 15, 16, 17, 18, 19, and 20 games for the N.Y. Giants.

236. He caught his first game with Toledo in 1884 and his last with Detroit in 1912.

237. After going 20–12 in 1970, this Cincinnati lefty crashed to 1–11 the following year.

238. Between 1948 and 1957 he drove in more runs than any player other than Stan Musial. He was Stan's teammate during the 1957 and 1958 campaigns.

239. Signed by the A's out of high school, this fine hitting pitcher was through after eleven seasons at only twenty-seven years of age.

240. Batting averages rose so drastically during the 1890s that this Hall of Famer failed to cop a crown despite going over the .400 mark in 1894 and 1895.

241. Winner of the most games in the N.L. during the forties, he was tagged 4F and exempted from duty in World War II because of a hunting accident that resulted in half his foot being shot off.

242. As a result of the strike-shortened 1994 season, he was the only pitcher to spin at least 200 innings.

243. Earlier in his life he did time for armed robbery but switched from stolen booty to stolen bases as he became the first player to lead both leagues in swiped sacks.

244. Try to recall the lefty who won 24 games in 1973 but retired with only 57 victories.

245. Once a league leader in dingers, this post-World War II third baseman hit all but 6 of his 160 homers while playing on a club for which he held the career clout record upon his retirement.

246. Name the outspoken swatter who led the N.L. in slugging during the sixties and the A.L. in that department in the seventies.

247. His .765 slugging average in 1927 is the highest for a league qualifier who failed to lead in that category.

248. Paul Molitor collected over 200 hits at age forty in 1996. Which Hall of Famer was the only other forty-year-old to reach this milestone?

249. After toiling for fourteen years exclusively with the Indians, he suited up for the Senators, Browns, Giants, as well as the Tribe, all in 1940.

250. Between 1968 and 1978 this hurler fanned over 200 batters in all but one season, missing by just four in 1977.

251. Alex Rodriguez made a name for himself in 1996 by posting incredible offensive numbers at shortstop. However, another man once drove in 159 runs at that position. Name him.

252. Leading the A.L. in ERA at the time of his trade from Texas to L.A. on August 19, 1983, his 2.42 mark was frozen and proved good enough for the title.

253. He won batting titles with averages of .381 and .390 in the thirties but failed to do so with marks of .384 and .392 in the twenties.

254. This Hall of Famer won a batting crown in the deadball era with a .335 mark but failed to win one during the twenties in spite of hitting .375 in successive seasons.

255. The single-season record for walks by a shortstop, a second sacker, and a third baseman are all held by players named Eddie. Name the trio.

256. Which Hall of Fame shortstop hit .222 as a regular in 1892 and .401 in 1896?

257. Can you name the lefty who holds the A.L. record for issuing the most walks in a season while posting an ERA below 2.00?

258. Considered the fiercest competitor of his time, he retired at the close of the 1975 campaign after spending an N.L. record seventeen seasons as a pitcher with the same club.

259. His 33 wins in 1904 represent the highest total by a man who failed to lead his league during the twentieth century. Name him and his Iron Man teammate who lead the way with 35 wins.

260. In 1988 this National Leaguer became the first batter to lead in hits and strikeouts in the same season.

261. The year 1988 saw him hit .313 to set the N.L. record for lowest average by a batting titlist. However, he has had many seasons where his numbers have far exceeded that mark.

262. Arizona State University has proved a breeding ground for future big league talent. Name the first man to play in their program who went on to the Hall of Fame.

263. The last surviving member of the N.L.'s inaugural season, he is the only pitcher since 1876 to win at least 40 games for three straight seasons.

264. In 1928 he became the only teenager in the twentieth century to bat at least 400 times and hit .300.

265. He holds the N.L. single-season record for hits by a third baseman and compiled 231 on two occasions.

266. Noted for his shaky glove work at first base, he is the only player to smack 200 into the seats in both the majors and the minors.

267. Not only was he the first African American to win a big league batting crown, he was also the first to do so in the minors three years earlier.

268. When George Brett battered A.L. pitching for a .390 average in 1980, he outhit this N.L. leader by 66 points.

269. Only once have two players representing the same city in different leagues won batting crowns while hitting .400 in a season. Name the players, the year, and the city where they starred.

270. As a regular in 1918, this infielder hit .195 with Connie Mack's crew. Two years later he delighted the Tall Tactician by climbing to .322.

271. Given the Hall of Fame nod in 1995, he was the only player in the fifties to collect 200 hits three times.

272. In 1996 he became the first southpaw to rack up 300 saves.

273. Although he began as a starter in the sixties, this closer saved more games than any other N.L. reliever during the seventies.

274. His season of 28 wins is the most among N.L. pitchers since World War II.

275. From 1935 to 1944 this half-Cherokee outfielder drove in more runs than any other player with the exception of Joe Medwick.

276. Between 1969 and 1970 he deposited 77 balls into the seats yet committed 67 miscues on the field.

277. He was the only player to slam at least 20 over the fence during the 1972 and 1981 strike-shortened seasons.

278. Which hurler started his first game during the Kennedy administration and his last when Bush was in office?

279. Hailing from Cuba, this pot-bellied hurler with a hesitation in his delivery won ERA titles with marks below 2.00 in the sixties and the seventies.

280. This Dominican fly chaser was the first big league batting champ to later play in Japan.

281. As a freshman in 1984, this squat A.L. outfielder batted 557 times without a homer, but went on to hit more than 200 over his next eleven seasons.

282. In just nine seasons of N.L. play this five-time 20-game winner of the deadball era committed more errors than any pitcher in either league during the twentieth century.

283. Born Miltiades Papastegios, he was the first pitcher to win 200 games without ever bagging 20 in a season.

284. After seven N.L. seasons in which he posted wins in the double figures during the 1980s, he spent two years in Japan and then returned to the majors, winning 20 in the A.L. in 1991.

285. Baseball's only 20-game winner in 1982 turned thirty-eight in December of that year.

286. Name the hurler who led the N.L. with 24 victories despite pitching for a team who finished eighth in a ten-club league.

287. He won at least 20 games six times between 1929 and 1936 while pitching for teams that finished higher than fourth only once.

288. In 1981 and 1982 this righty worked a combined 283 innings and fanned just 117 batters. In 1986 he exploded compiling over 300 strikeouts while pitching eight fewer innings than he logged in those two earlier seasons.

289. In 1979 the N.L. sported two 20-game winners who were brothers. Name these siblings.

290. He caught 150 games in 1996, but his father did him 10 games better in 1968.

291. Just one A.L. hurler won 20 games in a season during the fifties and the sixties. Name him.

292. Because of the level of competition during this batting champ's heyday, he had eight qualifying seasons when his batting average topped .350 but failed to lead his league each time.

293. Two players hit 49 homers in a season twice while never reaching 50 in any season. Name these Hall of Fame fence crushers.

294. When Lefty Grove won 31 games for the A's in 1931, he broke this southpaw's junior circuit record.

295. The first reliever to retire with over 100 saves while pitching for only one team was the single-season recordholder until 1983.

296. This A.L. fireman of the eighties was the first to save 200 games for one club yet faded so quickly he was reduced to a setup man by the Cards before the close of the decade.

297. Name the first player to hit 300 homers who later had a son break into the majors. Name his son, too.

298. His thirteen-year streak of 25 or more saves came to an end during the 1996 campaign.

299. The only regular DH to bat at least .300 in the maiden season of its deployment had once bagged consecutive batting crowns in the N.L.

300. In 1969 he hit a record 37 homers by the All-Star game but could only muster 10 more the rest of the way and failed to lead his league.

301. By early May of 1930 his career record stood at 39–96. However, a change of scenery turned him around and by 1967 he was in the Hall of Fame.

302. Dubbed the "Dutch Master," he was the only N.L. pitcher to fan at least 200 batters in a season during the forties.

303. Identify the last A.L. lefty to work at least 300 innings in one season.

304. The last man to complete at least 100 starts over a four-year period was elected to the Hall of Fame in 1991, eight years after his retirement.

305. Name the last A.L. pitcher to win at least 25 games in one season for a club that finished below .500.

306. Four years after securing the N.L. batting crown in 1947, he became the first former big league titlist in the twentieth century to win the triple-A equivalent when he served as player-manager of Columbus in the American Association.

307. Possessed with great speed, he nabbed 122 sacks combined during the 1990 and 1991 seasons yet failed to qualify for the batting title in either year.

308. In 1996 Lance Johnson became the first National Leaguer to slap at least 20 triples since this star in 1957.

309. Wildness plagued the career of this lefty who in 1951 became the first pitcher to walk at least 150 batters while averaging fewer than one inning for each scheduled game.

310. This Hall of Famer collected over 1,500 hits yet retired with a batting average below .270.

311. Having never pitched relief in over 200 major league games, this hurler was relegated to the pen in 1996 and then demoted to Triple-A Vancouver where he received his first taste of minor league ball.

312. Batting averages rose so sharply after the deadball era that this Cub outfielder's .263 mark was the lowest among all N.L. players who had at least 350 at-bats in 1925.

313. Between 1923 and 1927 these two brothers started against each other ten times, more than any other siblings in baseball history.

314. The first National Leaguer to fan at least 1,000 times was also the only batter other than Duke Snider to drive in more than 1,000 runs during the fifties.

315. In 1978 he became the first man to bat in all 162 scheduled games without ever playing in the field.

316. Two men who collected at least 100 hits in every season during the seventies averaged .300. Pete Rose is one. Name the other.

317. His 89 hits in 1970 blocked him from joining the players described above. However, he is the only other N.L. hitter besides Pete Rose who played throughout the seventies to collect at least 1,500 hits while averaging .300 during that period.

318. As a result of Philadelphia's awesome offense during the 1890s, he became the only pitcher to win at least 20 games while recording ERAs above 4.00 for three years running.

319. Of his 348 homers, all but his last came in the N.L.

320. Identify the first reliever to save at least 40 games in one season with three teams. Name the pitcher and the teams.

321. Pete Rose was the first switch-hitter to lead his league in hits for two straight years. This paunchy third sacker became the second in 1992.

322. Speed and agility did not prevent this star from committing more errors than any other outfielder who debuted since World War II.

323. The only receiver to catch at least 150 games for three consecutive years did it between 1968 and 1970.

324. At age thirty-eight he was the youngest 3,000-hit man to voluntarily retire from the majors.

325. He has the lowest career ERA for any 200-game winner who broke in since World War II.

326. His 96 steals were not enough to lead the N.L. in 1980.

327. He was the first hurler to retire with at least 250 wins who never had a season where his ERA went below 3.00.

328. All but seven of his 288 career homers were hit after he turned thirty-one in 1948.

329. The last reliever to lead his league with fewer than 20 saves was this Minnesota Twin who pocketed 18 at the age of thirty-nine in 1968.

330. From 1988 to 1993 this fireman appeared in at least 50 games in a season with five different teams.

331. After failing as a starter, he became the first N.L. lefty to save at least 40 games in one season.

332. In his final season at the age of forty-five, this Hall of Famer became the oldest player to collect at least 100 hits in one season.

333. This man cracked more homers in 1996 than any other lead-off batter in a season.

334. This speedy second baseman was the first middle infielder to fan at least 150 times in 1984.

335. Complications following appendicitis surgery during the 1949 season killed the only pitcher in the twentieth century to win more than 100 games while issuing fewer than 300 walks.

336. In 1996 who became the first player to pound at least 300 homers who began his career by cracking a four-bagger in his initial big league at-bat?

337. One of the game's greatest stars was also the first man to fan 1,000 times before his thirtieth birthday.

338. Since the creation of the save rule in 1969, he was the first National Leaguer to total 100 saves.

339. In 1922, at the age of thirty-five, he became the oldest regular to hit .400.

340. Closing out his career in 1979, he was the last pitcher to retire with over 200 wins who had never played in the minors.

341. The first pitcher to appear in at least 50 games in each season for ten straight years saw his streak come to an end in 1970.

342. In 1970 this native of Lacoochee, Florida, became the first man to save at least 20 games in one season who had previously led his league in wins as a starter.

343. Name the first forty year old to fan at least 200 batters in a season.

344. Between 1972 and 1979 Nolan Ryan was the A.L. strikeout leader in all but one season. Name the only other pitcher to top the junior circuit during this period.

345. Todd Hundley broke Roy Campanella's single-season record for most homers by a catcher in 1996. Fewer noticed when this player set the new A.L. standard at the same position later that month.

346. A line drive ruined the effectiveness of this big league 20-game winner, who had set the minor league American Association mark for strikeouts in a season with Indianapolis in 1954.

347. He was the first catcher to lead his league in RBI.

348. During the 1980s he was the only player to drive in at least 120 runs three times.

349. This Hall of Famer was the first pitcher to lead the A.L. in ERA for two teams.

350. Name the only man who played prior to the divisional setup who lead his league in batting while representing a last-place club.

351. His 40 career pinch hits are the most for any player who amassed at least 3,000 safeties.

352. When this man bowed out with the Phillies in 1976, he became the first batter to retire with over 1,000 strikeouts and fewer than 100 homers to his credit.

353. This stocky swinger had 100 RBI seasons for Cincinnati, Houston, and Baltimore in the same decade.

354. Given his first shot in 1971, this player proceeded to win at least 10 games in a season for six teams.

355. He won or shared A.L. home-run titles with totals of 39 and 46. But earlier in his professional career he failed to lead the Pacific Coast League despite pounding 51 with Sacramento in 1974.

356. Few today will recall the name of the 200-game winner and player-manager who drowned in Canada in 1911.

357. Name the Hall of Famer who lived sixty-nine years after he won his second batting crown with the Reds in 1919.

358. Another durable Hall of Famer died seventy-one years after leading the N.L. in RBI with the Phillies in 1900.

359. He died in 1985, seventy-three years after his 30-win season with the Red Sox.

360. The first 200-game winner to live to the age of ninety last saw action with the Braves in 1925.

361. Once a .400 hitter, he died at age ninety-two in 1989.

362. This Hall of Famer passed away with 270 victories to his credit at the age of ninety-two in 1985.

363. Who led his league in batting with a mark that proved to be 43 points below his career average?

364. A roommate of Babe Ruth and later a teammate of Dizzy Dean, this second baseman died at age ninety-two in 1994 while a member of the Angels' coaching staff.

365. This pioneer of using film to study and showcase baseball died at age ninety in 1989, seventy years after winning the A.L. batting crown.

366. Christy Mathewson died in Saranac Lake, New York, in 1925. Name his teammate of ten seasons who died in the same town forty-nine years later.

367. His .368 average while playing behind the dish for the Phillies would have led the N.L. in 1954 had the earlier qualifying rules been in effect.

368. Name the first native Californian to hit 500 homers.

369. The man who pounded the most career dingers for any player born in Florida also ended his career in the sunshine state.

370. Mickey Mantle topped this A.L. outfielder's 288 mark for the most clouts by an Oklahoman.

371. This Hall of Famer who hung it up after the 1976 season tops all Texans in taters.

372. His career total of seat reachers surpasses the nearest challenger from his home state by more than 500. Name this Hall of Famer born in Idaho.

373. Mel Ott knocked more over the fence than any player born in this state.

374. Prior to Dave Winfield, this player, who died from lymph gland cancer in 1985, was the leading fence blaster among Minnesotans.

375. He hit 47 doubles in 1996, breaking the single-season record for backstops.

376. Last active with the Giants in 1964, this 200-game winner retired needing only one more strikeout for 2,000.

377. The man who played with eight different teams for the Pacific Coast League during the first three decades of the twentieth century was also called on to replace banned Black Sox third baseman Buck Weaver in 1921.

378. Name the first N.L. switch-hitter to win a batting title.

379. Texas had its first batting champ with this man.

380. This Canadian-born Hall of Famer broke in with the Phillies in 1965.

381. Lewis was the given name of this Hall of Fame outfielder who debuted with the New York Giants in 1923.

382. The Oakland A's gave this Hall of Fame second baseman his last shot in 1984.

383. One of the game's greatest position players got his first taste of the bigs with Louisville in 1897.

384. Babe Ruth bowed out with this inept team in 1935.

385. He threw his last big league pitch with San Francisco in 1965 and was elected to the Hall eight years later.

386. Chicago Cub fans saw this Hall of Fame pitcher's last hurrah in 1966.

387. After eighteen years with Brooklyn, this Hall of Fame outfielder closed his career with the Philadelphia A's in 1927.

388. While Mark McGwire was making a name for himself as a rookie in 1987, this Hall of Fame teammate was taking his final cuts.

389. This Hall of Fame shortstop broke in with Pittsburgh in 1926.

390. By the time this Hall of Famer toiled for Walt Alston in 1975, there were no more wins left in his weary arm.

391. His Hall of Fame career came to a close with Cleveland in 1955 after averaging nearly 37 homers a season.

392. Name the southpaw who saw his Hall of Fame career come to an end after starting and losing his only game with Washington in 1943.

393. The last clout of his Hall of Fame career came in a Brewer uniform in 1976.

394. A year after hitting just .246 at second with the Philadelphia A's in 1916, this Hall of Famer guided Toronto of the International League to a pennant and led the circuit with a .380 average.

395. This reliever appeared in his 1,070 and last game during his stint with the Dodgers in 1972.

396. After nineteen years with Washington, this outfielder took his curtain call with Cleveland in 1934.

397. A two-time .400 hitter, he called it quits after the 1930 season with the Boston Braves.

398. The Flatbush faithful saw this slugger take his final cuts with San Francisco in 1964.

399. Which Hall of Fame third baseman was last seen with Baltimore in 1957?

400. He was named manager of the Reds in 1916 and also toiled the last inning of his Hall of Fame career that season.

401. Once a 40-game winner, this great White Sox spitballer took the mound for the last time after joining the Boston Braves in 1917.

402. This member of the 500-homer club was killed in an auto accident on November 21, 1958.

403. Another 500-dinger man died in 1967 after choking on a piece of meat.

404. Minnesota was the last stop for this 300-game winner in 1987.

405. His 390th and final homer came with Montreal in 1988.

406. Elected to the Hall in 1945, this third baseman snagged his last grounder in 1908 as a member of the Philadelphia A's.

407. He returned to the Braves in 1989 after a thirteen-year hiatus for the final year of his career and retired with 414 dingers.

408. Name this native of Puerto Rico who hit 30 homers in 1964 without playing more than 48 games at any one position.

409. Ty Cobb took the field for the last time as a member of this team in 1928.

410. The Kansas City A's handed this venerable fifty-nine-year-old hurler the ball for one game in 1965.

411. Richie Ashburn left the game after batting .306 for this first-year expansion team.

412. This Hall of Famer caught his last game with the New York Giants in 1941 after having played the previous nineteen seasons with the Cubs.

413. Dave Winfield ended his career with this powerhouse team in 1995.

414. Over 300 wins were accumulated by this man, who died in an insane asylum on February 4, 1909.

415. These two men picked up their 300th wins in 1985.

416. He began his pitching career in 1963, but did not record the first of three 20-win seasons until 1977.

417. Name the receiver who caught for Baltimore at three separate junctures during his career in the 1970s.

418. Identify the two-time batting champ who fanned over 1,500 times.

419. His 10,654 at-bats are the most for any player who did not attain 3,000 hits.

420. Cuba's first representative to win 20 games in one season was this man, who led the N.L. with 27 for Cincinnati in 1923.

421. After having spent the last seven seasons in Japan, this former Expo outfielder returned for his last big league fling with the Royals in 1991.

422. He led the A.L. in singles in 1990 and belted 39 homers six years later.

423. This graceful fielder, who was last seen with the Red Sox in 1934, is the only American Leaguer to play 20 seasons at first base.

424. When this slugger belted 26 homers in 1977, he poled them with four different teams. Name him and the clubs.

425. In 1988 the Cardinals used this native of Puerto Rico at all nine positions during the season. The following year he became the first Redbird to play 163 games in one season.

426. The three-game N.L. playoff tacked on to the regular season in 1962 enabled this speedster to become the only man to appear in 165 games.

427. Winner of 193 games, he cracked 38 homers, more than any other pitcher in history.

428. Never too shy to dust a batter off, this Hall of Fame hurler popped 7 homers in 1958 and again in 1965.

429. Between 1969 and 1978 this well-traveled outfielder hit over 30 homers six times yet never reached 40 in a single season.

430. His 30 homers during the 1996 season made him the first A.L. player to hit that many six times without ever reaching 40 homers.

431. Ten of this "Capitol Punisher's" A.L.-leading 44 clouts in 1968 came during one torrid week in May.

432. He led the N.L. in RBI each year from 1976 to 1978 yet never drove in 100 in any other season.

433. Who fanned at least 100 times in a season on eighteen occasions in his career?

434. Over 300 wins were picked up by this man, who also set an N.L. record when he led or tied his league in losses from 1977 to 1980.

435. This man walked at least 100 times for a record seven straight seasons between 1936 and 1942.

436. In 1930 appendicitis kept this Hall of Famer out of the lineup until June, reducing his hit total to just 94 after averaging 226 safeties over his first three seasons.

437. A notorious headhunter, this 300-game winner had five 20-win seasons, all of them coming after he turned thirty.

438. After having been a fixture for nineteen years with the Red Sox, this outfielder played his final season with Baltimore in 1991.

439. En route to his 373 victories, he beat the Reds a record 70 times between 1911 and 1930.

440. When this slugger paced the A.L. with 46 homers in 1936, he established an all-time mark by pounding 14 of them against Cleveland.

441. No player scored more career runs for the Red Sox than this man.

442. The first native of Mexico to pound 40 homers in a season was this N.L. third baseman in 1996.

443. In 1996 Ellis Burks became the first National Leaguer to whack 40 homers and collect 200 hits in the same season since this man in 1970.

444. In 1978 he became the first player to lead the majors in homers, ribbies, and triples in the same season.

445. This first-ballot Hall of Famer reached double figures in homers just twice during his twenty-four-year career.

446. Elected to the Hall in 1949, this man recorded ERAs below 1.50 four years running, starting in 1906.

447. During this Hall of Fame shortstop's twenty-three-year career he never batted .300 or hit more than five homers in a season.

448. Born William O'Kelleher, he retired with a record eight straight 200-hit seasons to his credit.

449. This man was enshrined in Cooperstown as a manager but was also the first switch-hitter to draw 1,000 walks.

450. Longevity marked the career of this man, who bagged his first win at age eighteen for the A's in 1912 and his last win at age forty for the Red Sox in 1934.

451. Nearly four seasons of this man's career were spent in the Navy during World War II, costing him a chance at 300 wins and at Walter Johnson's career strikeout record.

452. The first N.L. player to crack as many as 47 homers who failed to top his league fell 4 shy of leading in 1955.

453. Prior to Tony Gwynn's two streaks of three straight batting titles, who was the last National Leaguer to take top honors for three straight seasons?

454. Name the 500-homer man whose brother Rich played 57 games at first for San Francisco during the 1980s.

455. George was the given name of this Yankee Hall of Famer's brother who caught for the Red Sox and White Sox during the thirties and forties. Name the Yankee sibling.

456. Three hundred seventy-three wins are on the slate of this man whose brother Henry walked 14 batters in his only big league start in 1906.

457. Owner of a .305 lifetime average while playing for one club over twenty-one seasons, his brother Ken toiled for ten teams in fourteen years.

458. Younger brother Tommie's 13 homers represent less than 2 percent of this man's total.

459. Luke played six more seasons than his brother who was elected to the Hall of Fame in 1977. A third sibling named Tommy snuck into one game with the Cubs in 1927.

460. This infielder was briefly managed by his Hall of Fame father in 1985.

461. Earl Jr. bounced around with five teams during the fifties and sixties with the hope of following in this man's footsteps.

462. Another junior was this outfielder named Eddie, whose career hit total fell more than 3,200 short of his dad's.

463. While piloting a team he owned, this Hall of Famer managed his son Earle during a few token games between 1910 and 1914.

464. Unlike his durable sibling, Billy has never played a full slate of games in one season.

465. Name the Hall of Fame second baseman who was adored by Red Sox fans for fourteen seasons.

466. He began his Hall of Fame career sharing the Browns' catching duties with Wally Schang in 1929.

467. Although he never hit .300 during an eighteen-year catching career that began in 1946, he did win a batting title with Baltimore in the International League the year before his major league debut.

468. In 1955 Cooperstown called for a man who pitched twenty-one years in the majors without ever having played in the minors or on a pennant winner. Name him.

469. The Giants sold this Hall of Famer and future batting champ to Cleveland despite a .309 average in his rookie season in 1890.

470. Name the Hall of Famer who debuted as a position player with Buffalo in 1880 and averaged more than 28 wins over the following eleven seasons.

471. Kansas City was the last stop on the line for this 300-game winner in 1983.

472. Hazen was the given name of this Hall of Fame outfielder whose career came to a close with Brooklyn in 1938.

473. Which former slugging star ended his career by clubbing only 5 homers in 310 at-bats for the pennant-winning Cardinals in 1968?

474. All 235 of his career homers, including his back-to-back N.L.-leading totals during World War II, came after he left the Philadelphia A's.

475. All of Joe Carter's homers came after he departed the team with which he made his debut in 1983. Identify the club.

476. Former big leaguer Frank was eighteen years younger than his Hall of Fame brother, who was last spotted with the Pirates in 1939.

477. A year before the Cards called up this Hall of Fame outfielder, he tore up the minor league American Association with Columbus, leading all other players with a .382 average.

478. Five big league batting titles were on the way for this man, who won his first hitting crown in organized ball for Pawtucket of the International League in 1981.

479. Name the colorful 30-game winner whose given name was Jay.

480. After the completion of this Hall of Famer's sixth season in 1933, his career average stood at a whopping .359. Thereafter, he tailed off dramatically, averaging only .277 during his final eleven campaigns.

481. What was the second highest homer total for all-time single-season recordholder Roger Maris during his major league career?

482. Retiring with a .344 average, he outhit every other player who collected 2,000 safeties without ever attaining 200 in one season.

483. Boston proved forgiving when they let this man return in 1990, making him a four-decade player.

484. His 2,581 games at short are the most for any other man, regardless of position, who never played anywhere else on the diamond.

485. He spent his entire Hall of Fame career in the Yankees outfield yet never popped more than 9 homers in any one season.

486. This man, who played over 1,000 games each at short and in the outfield, also had an older brother who relieved in one game for Houston in 1971.

487. Seven batting championships went to this man, who played over 1,000 games both at second and at first.

488. In 1970 he became the first A.L. shortstop to whack 40 homers in one season.

489. He collected the first of six 200-hit seasons at the age of thirty-two in 1929.

490. The Yankees' single-season record for steals stood for seventy years until this man was acquired prior to the start of the 1985 season.

491. Joe Sewell replaced the only player to collect 1,000 hits who died before turning thirty.

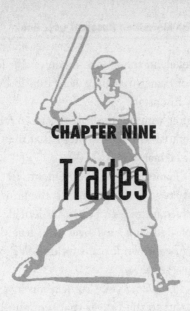

CHAPTER NINE

Trades

1. This man, who played all six games at the hot corner for the Cards in the 1930 Series, was involved in trades for Kiki Cuyler and Leo Durocher.

2. When the Yankees traded for Jim Abbott, one of the players they sent to the Angels became the only switch-hitter to drive in 100 runs during the 1995 season.

3. One of the pitchers the Twins received in exhange for Frank Viola went on to save over 200 games.

4. On August 12, 1987, the Tigers went for a quick fix when they sent this hurler to Atlanta for Doyle Alexander.

5. Which 200-game winner was involved in trades for home-run champs Rocky Colavito and Dick Allen?

6. A major run producer, he was involved in a deal for Sandy Alomar in 1989, only to be shipped to another team with his brother Roberto the following season.

7. Many fans know the Mets received Jim Fregosi for Nolan Ryan. But can you name the three players New York sent along to the Angels with Ryan to sweeten the deal?

8. By 1939 Cleveland thought so much of this former star and future Hall of Famer that they dealt him to Detroit straight-up for Harry Eisenstat.

9. Four years after winning the batting crown for the Tribe, his skills deteriorated to such an extent that the Orioles nabbed him for Russ Heman and $30,000.

10. This Hall of Famer preferred retirement after the 1956 season rather than adding his name to the growing roll call of players involved in trades for Dick Littlefield.

11. The cries of Red Sox fans over the deal that sent Larry Andersen to Beantown for this future MVP only build with each passing season.

12. In November of 1923, Casey Stengel was involved in a trade from the Giants to the Braves that sent another future Hall of Famer to Boston to serve as a player-manager. What is his name?

13. Red Barrett won 2 games for the Braves in 1945 and then 21 more after he was sent to the Cards in late May. Which former three-time 20-game winner did Boston receive?

14. After a 2–19 showing with the Pirates in 1985, Jose Deleon was shipped to the White Sox during the 1986 campaign. The player who went the other way has since posted four 100-RBI seasons. What is his name?

15. Phillie fans now lament the winter of 1982 when Larry Bowa and this future star were moved to Wrigley for Ivan DeJesus.

16. Six days after the 1965 World Series ended, the Mets swapped Charlie Smith and Al Jackson for a player who had won an MVP the previous year.

17. Although Johnny Sain was a good pickup for the Yankees during the pennant drive of 1951, Bomber fans would love to have kept this future 200-game winner whom they gave away in the exchange.

18. Nicknamed the "Hoosier Thunderbolt," his fireballing right arm was shot by the time the faltering Reds got him in exchange for Christy Mathewson during the off-season of 1900.

19. After being dealt for five guys and a quarter of a million dollars, he responded with 41 homers in his first season with Atlanta.

20. Rather than report to the New York Giants with Johnny Allen, this former Brooklyn MVP retired during the 1943 season. He resurfaced in 1945 with the Red Sox.

21. Just two years after winning the N.L. batting crown, his stock had fallen so low that he was sent to Texas straight up for Jim Panther.

22. When Atlanta traded former N.L. MVP Orlando Cepeda to Oakland, which former A.L. MVP did they get in return?

23. George Scott and Bernie Carbo were dealt to the Boston Red Sox after the 1976 season for which future star?

24. The Indians thought this Hall of Fame righty was through when they shipped him to the nation's capital for Byron Speece and Carr Smith in 1924.

25. Three years after winning the MVP award, this man was sent to Cleveland for Bill Davis in October of 1968.

26. Seven years prior to winning the Cy Young, he was traded in a package deal for Joe Morgan. Three years after winning the award, he was traded straight up for Juan Berenguer.

27. The Dodgers bid adieu to Willie Davis when they traded for this hurler, who went on to set a single-season record for pitching appearances that still stands.

28. A season after securing the Rookie of the Year, the Dodgers swapped him and Bob Stinson for Dick Allen.

29. Which two-time A.L. home-run champ was involved in trades for Tito Francona twice during the late fifties?

30. Rick Wise was twice involved in transactions for pitchers who would later win the Cy Young. Name the two mounds-men.

31. Which slugger did the Angels acquire when they dealt Mickey Rivers and Ed Figueroa to the Bronx?

32. This former star was traded twice during the sixties and was the immediate managerial replacement for both teams.

33. The Yankees were so eager to nab Ken Phelps from Seattle they cast off this slugging outfielder in a package deal.

34. Which big league great was traded by the Expos for Tom Lawless in 1984?

35. The writing was on the wall for this 300-game winner when he was traded straight up for Steve Lyons in 1986.

36. Brooklyn traded Dutch Ruether to Cincinnati for which for-mer Giant mainstay?

37. Which Hall of Famer was traded twice during the 1941 season?

38. On December 13, 1934, the Gas House Gang sold this minor leaguer to the Reds, only to have him returned because of an injury. He broke in to the big leagues two years later and was elected to the Hall in 1981.

39. Football Hall of Famer Greasy Neale was traded from Cincinnati with Jimmy Ring for which future Hall of Fame pitcher?

40. This 300-game winner was dealt to the Yankees with Del Pratt in January of 1918. However, he quit without ever appearing for New York.

41. Winning the batting crown didn't keep this player from being traded the following year to the New York Giants for Hugh Poland and Connie Ryan.

42. In 1916 the Giants received Buck Herzog and Red Killefer from Cincinnati for this trio of future Hall of Famers.

43. Looking to fill their gap at second, the Red Sox unloaded Albie Pearson and Norm Zauchin on Washington for a hitter who would go on to bag a pair of batting crowns.

44. On March 15, 1978, Charlie O. Finley continued his quest to break up the A's when he sent this former star to Candlestick for seven players and a chunk of change.

45. The Bosox acquired this outfield star when they dumped Mickey McDermott and Tom Umphlett on the Senators.

46. In his first year with Cleveland this player won his sixth stolen-base title after being swapped for Jeff Heath.

47. A solid hitter for seventeen seasons, he was packaged in separate deals for the fathers of Barry Bonds and Ken Griffey Jr.

48. A year after Washington handed this guy over to the Red Sox for Bill Barrett, he hit a record 67 doubles.

49. The Redbirds said farewell to a fading Whitey Lockman in exhange for this righty, who hung it up fifteen years later.

50. Darold Knowles, Bob Locker, and Manny Trillo went from the A's to the Cubs for this aging former star.

51. Moose Skowron switched teams with this L.A. Dodger pitcher who a month earlier had lost the final game of the N.L. playoffs in 1962.

52. Four years after winning an MVP award, this player was sent to the Pirates for Bob Bailey and Gene Michael.

53. He thrilled the fans at Fenway with 119 ribbies after coming over from Detroit for Eddie Lake in 1946.

54. Tony Scott was sent to Houston for this volatile hurler, who would post back-to-back 20-win seasons for Whitey Herzog.

55. Although never traded, this 400-home-run hitter signed as a free agent with three different clubs.

56. In addition to Joe De Maestri and Kent Hadley, whom did the Yankees receive when they shipped a quartet of players to the A's in December 1959?

57. Houston made a major blunder when they packaged this lefty to Baltimore for Curt Blefary and a minor leaguer.

58. He starred for years with Milwaukee after Cincinnati dealt him for Rocky Bridges and cash.

59. He was the principal player acquired by the Cards from the Cubs in exhange for Ernie Broglio and two others.

60. Believe it or not, all Detroit needed to give up for this first baseman was Steve Demeter, who played only four games with Cleveland before departing for good after the 1960 season.

61. In June of 1993 Jeff Darwin was packaged in a deal that sent him from Seattle to Florida for this injury-plagued third baseman. Five months later, Darwin was traded back to Seattle straight up for this same player.

62. The Reds pulled a fast one on San Francisco when they traded Vern Geishert and Frank Duffy for this power hitter.

63. Little did the Seattle Pilots know that they were handing this Rookie of the Year over to the Royals for John Gelnar and Steve Whitaker.

64. Mets' fans still shiver when reminded of the outfielder they dealt for Joe Foy.

65. Joe Gordon and Eddie Bockman went to the Indians for this hurler, who came through in the clutch many times for Casey Stengel.

66. The Cardinals traded this reigning batting champion to Cincinnati for Harvey Hendrick, Benny Frey, and some cash in 1932.

67. A year later, Harvey Hendrick was in another package deal that sent him from the Cubs to the Phillies for a slugger who had won the Triple Crown that season.

68. One of the all-time great steals occurred when the White Sox sent Braggo Roth and two obscure players to the Indians for this great lefty-swinging outfielder.

69. Connie Mack gave up on this Hall of Famer and shuttled him to Detroit for Barney McCosky.

70. After the 1956 season, this lefty was sitting on top of the world. Four years later the Tribe traded him straight up to the White Sox for Barry Latman.

71. This great shortstop went from Washington to the Bosox for Lyn Lary and $225,000.

72. A future Hall of Famer, he played his final season in an Indians' uniform, coming over in the deal that sent Gene Woodling to the Pirates.

73. After fourteen seasons at Wrigley the Cubs dealt this former star to their crosstown rivals for Steve Stone and three others.

74. Do you remember who the Mets got from San Francisco for Charlie Williams and cash in 1972?

75. A real coup for the Yanks, this player was acquired from Boston for Danny Cater.

76. In his first year back with San Francisco after he was dealt from Washington for Cap Peterson and Bob Priddy, this man proceeded to win the Cy Young Award.

77. The Cardinals acquired this future batting champ and MVP from the Yankees for Bob Sykes during the 1981 World Series.

78. The Indians picked up this vital cog in their pennant machine from the O's for minor leaguer Kyle Washington on All-Star game day in 1992.

79. Who is Bruce Ellingsen? Just the guy the Dodgers foisted on the Indians for this future star outfielder in 1974.

80. Boston gambled on their future when they sent Curt Schilling and this future standout to Baltimore for Mike Boddicker.

81. Little did the Red Sox know they were gift wrapping a future Hall of Famer to the Yanks for Cedric Durst and cash in 1930.

82. Washington stole this slugging outfielder from Baltimore for Gil Coan two months before the opening of the 1954 season.

83. In December 1933 John Stone was sent to Washington from Detroit for this veteran star who proved he could still produce.

84. Name the skipper who was managing in 1996 and who was involved in a package deal for Reggie Jackson.

85. Although Rick Sutcliffe paid immediate dividends for the Cubs, the outfielder they whisked away in this June 1984 trade would have provided thrills for years to come.

86. Pittsburgh named him their manager after dealing Manny Sanguillen along with $100,000 to Oakland.

87. The Chisox caught Connie Mack napping when they pilfered this future star with amazing bat control for Joe Tipton after the 1949 season.

88. In 1978 this forty year old showed he still had what it takes by leading the N.L. in wins with San Diego after arriving in a trade from Texas for Dave Tomlin and $125,000.

89. This mound ace left Detroit after he and Gus Triandos were acquired by the Phils for Don Demeter and Jack Hamilton.

90. Ellis Valentine flopped in the deal that brought him from the Expos to the Mets in 1981. What relief star did the Expos receive in the deal?

91. Pittsburgh cast off this Cooperstown-bound infielder to Brooklyn for "Hot Potato" Hamlin and three others after the 1941 season.

92. A batting championship was garnered by this standout in his first year with Cleveland. He came over from the Red Sox in a 1916 deal for Sad Sam Jones, Fred Thomas, and cash.

93. This future Hall of Famer had nothing but a tired arm when Brooklyn dispatched him and Gordon Slade to the Cards for Jake Flowers and Ownie Carroll.

94. Twins fans were unhappy when this popular outfielder was traded to the Cards for Tommy Herr.

95. Oakland acquired this future Cy Young winner in a package deal for Alfredo Griffin and Jay Howell.

96. This Beantown brother battery was traded together with Mel Almada to Washington for Ben Chapman and Bobo Newsom.

97. Mike Witt bombed with the Bombers after he came over from California in May 1990 in exchange for this outfielder.

98. The Royals exchanged Jim York and Lance Clemons to Houston for this burly slugger and a minor leaguer in the winter of 1971.

99. Cleveland received this waning all-time great from the Red Sox for Charlie Chech, Jack Ryan, and cash two months before the start of the 1909 season.

100. This superstar of the early thirties was a shell of his former self by the time the Cubs acquired him for Curt Davis, two others, and plenty of greenbacks.

CHAPTER TEN
National Association

1. Which Hall of Famer won over 200 games in the National Association?

2. An architect of the game's formative years, this man won pennants in each of the N.A.'s final four seasons.

3. This man not only managed Philadelphia to a pennant in the N.A.'s inaugural season of 1871, he won all of his team's games as a pitcher.

4. A future 3,000-hit man, he debuted with Rockford in 1871.

5. Name the Irish-born Boston outfielder who played the most career games in the N.A.

6. Three cities remained in the N.A. throughout its five-year run. Each were later represented in the National League's initial season. Name the cities.

7. Which 300-game winner threw his first big league pitch for the St. Louis Reds in 1875?

8. This city in upstate New York was represented in the N.A.'s first two seasons and later in the N.L.

9. Which player, who managed throughout the N.A.'s existence, was known as "Death to Flying Things"?

10. The hurler who won all of the New York Mutuals games in 1871 hailed from the Netherlands. Name this righty whose real first name was Reinder.

CHAPTER ELEVEN

Negro Leagues

1. The Newark Eagles won the championship in 1946 with a double play team who later played in the majors. Their second sacker hit over 250 homers in the majors, and their shortstop is in the Hall, but they both played other positions in the majors.

2. The father of an ill-fated major league namesake was an All-Star for the Birmingham Black Barons in 1941. Name him.

3. What was the given first name of speedster Cool Papa Bell?

4. Before he cracked over 500 homers in the majors, he played for the Kansas City Monarchs in 1950.

5. Which great shortstop, who had a career that spanned twenty-one years, was nicknamed "Devil"?

6. This third baseman and Pacific Coast League star was elected to the Hall of Fame in 1987.

7. Twenty-one years after he broke in with the Birmingham Black Barons, this man threw his first pitch in a major league World Series.

8. From which Negro League powerhouse team did Branch Rickey snatch Jackie Robinson?

9. This lefty-swinging Indianapolis native rode his twenty-six-year career into the Hall in 1976.

10. Sadly, this Newark Eagle standout died a week after his election to Cooperstown in 1995.

11. Name the Hall of Famer who spent six years with the Baltimore Elite Giants and another in Mexico before embarking on his ten-year big league career?

12. This Alabama-based team sported the letters "BBB" on their caps.

13. Elected to the Hall of Fame in 1977, this Cuban starred in Latin America as well as in the Negro Leagues.

14. A legend with the Pittsburgh Crawfords and the Homestead Grays, this catcher was given the Hall of Fame nod in 1972.

15. Nicknamed "Pop," this left-handed place hitter is generally regarded as the greatest player of color during the first two decades of the twentieth century.

16. Who was the first living former Negro Leaguer to be enshrined in Cooperstown who had never played in the majors?

17. Weighing in at 150 pounds, this Hall of Fame third baseman was in his prime while with the Philadelphia Hilldales during the 1920s.

18. These two Hall of Fame half-brothers from Calvert, Texas, were born nearly twenty-six years apart. No siblings who played in the major leagues can match this disparity.

19. An eleven-year veteran of Negro League ball, this Cuban hurler fathered a namesake who would win over 200 games in the majors.

20. This first baseman spent all but one of his twelve seasons with the Kansas City Monarchs. In 1962 the Cubs named him the first officially recognized African-American coach in the major leagues.

CHAPTER TWELVE

The World Series and Championship Playoffs

1. The first twentieth-century pitcher to bag two wins in back-to-back World Series picked up 300 in regular season play.

2. He became the first man to play in consecutive Series with a different team when he appeared in the 1915 classic as a Phillie after suiting up for the Braves the previous year.

3. Who pitched in Fall Classics in the seventies, eighties, and nineties?

4. Who was the first lefty to win two games in one World Series?

5. A native of Venezuela, his two Triple-A batting crowns were earned fifteen years apart. In the bigs he played in four Fall Classics during the seventies and was on winning teams in both leagues. Name him.

6. When was the last year a World Series game was played in September?

7. Who played all five games for the A's at second in 1905 and was then an outfielder five years later?

8. In the eight Series the Yankees played between 1956 and 1964, Whitey Ford started the first game in all but one. Who was the only other man to get a Game 1 starting nod?

9. After failing to homer in 540 at-bats for the White Sox in 1993, he waited until the playoffs to reach the seats.

10. As the result of Reggie Jackson's hamstring pull, which two players were summoned to plug the hole in center for Oakland during the 1972 Series?

11. Phil Rizzuto replaced the man who had the lowest career average with at least 100 at-bats in Series' play.

12. Prior to his 1995 assignment, a record sixteen years had passed since the last time this pitcher started a Fall Classic.

13. Who started the first game for the Reds against the Yankees in the 1976 Series and then took the hill in the opening game for the Bombers the following year?

14. When Johnny Evers broke his leg in 1910, which future Triple Crown winner took his place in the Series?

15. As a rookie infielder with Washington in 1925, this future batting champ collected as many hits in the Series as he did during the regular season.

16. He batted as a DH in the Series with Boston in 1986, Minnesota in 1987, and Oakland in 1988.

17. Serving as the Bombers' regular backstop in 1921, he became the last man to catch in all eight games of a nine-game Series.

18. Which war year featured the only World Series played entirely in September?

19. He started the most World Series games for any pitcher who never wore a New York uniform.

20. Two outfielders who played all eight games of the 1903 World Series did not live out the decade. Both led their respective teams in batting during the Series. Name this pair.

21. Both of Pittsburgh's homers in the 1909 Series were hit by this player-manager.

22. Ten ribbies in a six-game set weren't enough to lift his team over the L.A. Dodgers in 1959.

23. He dropped two games in one Series to McGraw's Giants by the score of 1–0.

24. Who played in the World Series for the Phillies in both 1983 and 1993?

25. Not only was he the winner in the Ruth "called shot" game, but he later went on to umpire in the Fall Classic.

26. Name the only position player to appear in League Championship Series (LCS) action during the sixties, seventies, and eighties.

27. In 1976, when Cincinnati's Dan Driessen became the first National Leaguer to bat in the DH slot in the history of the World Series, who did Sparky Anderson drop to ninth in the batting order throughout the contest?

28. Name the only pitcher to toss shutouts in three consecutive World Series.

29. This Hall of Famer made the final out in the first modern-day World Series in 1903.

30. At age eighteen the youngest player ever to appear in a World Series touched up Walter Johnson for 4 hits in one Series game.

31. The last pitcher to win 3 games in a World Series notched the third by defeating the man who turned the trick the year before. Name both pitchers.

32. Although Carl Hubbell won 24 straight regular season games between 1936 and 1937, he was defeated by this Yankee during the 1936 Series.

33. No starter has won 3 games in one League Championship Series, but this reliever bagged a trio during the NLCS of 1986.

34. Even fans of recent baseball history might struggle to retrieve the name of the Venezuelan who started 2 games in one World Series during the 1980s yet retired with only 10 wins.

35. He won the game in which Reggie Jackson blasted 3 straight homers to give the Yanks their first World Championship in fifteen years in 1977.

36. This reigning N.L. batting champ sat out the deciding game of the 1931 Series after injuring a fingernail when he dropped a fly ball.

37. Fred Clarke gave him the starting nod a record five times during the 1903 series.

38. Part Creek Indian, this hurler is the only man to win a World Series game in five consecutive seasons.

39. Name the Reds' outfielder who ripped A's pitching at a .750 clip only to be removed after being hit on the hand in the opening frame of the fourth and final game in 1990.

40. His 6$\frac{1}{3}$ innings of one-hit relief earned him the win for Pittsburgh in the first World Series night game in 1971.

41. Although he batted only .196 over 108 regular season games in 1988, this Dodger outfielder walked prior to Kirk Gibson's game-winning homer in the opening contest and then popped a dinger of his own in Game 5.

42. One of the game's greatest left arms belonged to the only man to fashion two extra-inning complete wins in World Series play.

43. This Yankee had the unique experience of pitching in the Series in each of his first four seasons between 1955 and 1958.

44. Oakland employed this reliever's services in all seven of their games against the Mets in 1973.

45. Tom Glavine and Mark Wohlers spun the first combined World Series one-hitter in 1995. The only hit allowed was to this thirty-eight-year-old Cleveland veteran.

46. Sporting two starters who later made the Hall of Fame, this team was nonetheless defeated in the 1971 NLCS by Pittsburgh in 4 games. Name the team and its Cooperstown-bound moundsmen.

47. This hill ace was downed by Yankee bats four times without a win during the forties and fifties.

48. Who started World Series games for the Royals, Reds, and the Phillies?

49. In 1985 he appeared in 74 games, all in relief. He would lose in a starting role during the 1989 Fall Classic.

50. Although he appeared in only one game in both the 1951 and 1952 classics, this Yankee lefty recorded the final outs in each Series.

51. Not to be outdone, this Reds' reliever repeated the above man's feat when he closed out the 1975 and 1976 classics.

52. As a rookie he threw his first complete game with the Yankees in Game 5 of the 1978 Series, after requiring relief assistance in all of his 22 regular-season starts.

53. This Yankee, who started game one of the 1976 Series, was not called upon to pitch during that year's championship series.

54. The youngest man to pitch a complete game shutout in the World Series played in Fall Classics with the same club during the sixties, seventies, and eighties.

55. His .227 average during the 1992 series was a vast improvement over his .045 showing in 1981.

56. He played regularly on all five A.L. pennant-winning teams between 1921 and 1939 that did not represent Philadelphia or New York.

57. Name the player who hit 4 homers in a World Series while batting in the seventh slot in the batting order.

58. This lefty toiled for Pittsburgh in the 1960 Series and in the 1970 NLCS.

59. Babe Ruth was on the team that set the record for the lowest World Series batting average posted by a winning team. Identify the team and year.

60. They rang the N.L. champ's pitching to the tune of .338 but lost the Series.

61. The only third baseman to play in as many as six World Series also coached pro hoops in the Basketball Association of America.

62. Reggie Jackson knocked three out of the park in Game 6 of the 1977 World Series, but this man performed that feat in 1926 and again in 1928.

63. In the 1992 NLCS, he became the first starter to drop 3 decisions.

64. Identify the Royals' reliever who served up the series-winning homer to New York's Chris Chambliss in the final game of the 1976 ALCS.

65. This red-headed outfielder was not only the first player to lead his league in hits three years running, but he was also the initial batter in the first modern World Series of 1903.

66. Name the pitcher who won 31 games during the regular season and popped a four-bagger during the Fall Classic.

67. Earl Weaver started this Oriole 20-game winner once during the 1971 Series and pressed him into a relief role in 3 other games.

68. This Hall of Famer was the first shortstop to pop a homer in World Series play.

69. Named after the President of the Confederacy, this man pitched in all four of Detroit's World Series appearances between 1934 and 1945.

70. He was given the gate after fanning 10 times while holding down the first-base job for Pittsburgh during the 1909 Series.

71. Roy Campanella was the first former Negro Leaguer to catch in a major league World Series. This Cuban was the second in 1951.

72. Try and recall the name of the man who pitched in World Series play for Sparky Anderson's first pennant winner in 1970 and his last in 1984.

73. One of the toughest competitors of his era, he saw action against the Yanks at the hot corner in both 1955 and 1960 when the Bombers lost to Brooklyn and Pittsburgh respectively.

74. Only one man pitched in the divisional playoffs in 1981 and 1996. Name him.

75. Postseason success rarely followed this infielder, who played in eight NLCS and emerged on the winning side just once, in 1971.

76. Mickey Lolich handed Bob Gibson his second loss in World Series play, snapping his seven-game winning streak. Name the Yankee rookie who handed Gibson his only other defeat.

77. The Pirate whose wild pitch brought the 1927 World Series to a close had his debut with Pittsburgh in the Federal League twelve years earlier.

78. He beat the Yankees as both a Brooklyn and an L.A. Dodger.

79. This San Francisco Giant outfielder cracked homers in each of the first 4 games of the NLCS in 1987.

80. Name the two-time 20-game winners who started a pair of games for the Giants in the 1921 Series yet logged only $2^2/3$ innings combined.

81. This Hall of Famer downed Brooklyn three times with Cleveland in the 1920 Series and died at the age of ninety-four in 1984.

82. A teammate of the man above, this Hall of Famer played all 7 games at short and died seventy years later at age ninety-one.

83. A third man on that club played each game at second, turned an unassisted triple play in the Series, and lived to talk about it until the age of ninety-one in 1985.

84. Name the only team to beat the Yankees in consecutive Fall Classics.

85. The only time both World Series combatants hit under .200 during the Fall Classic, the winning team had 23 fewer regular season victories than the loser. Name the teams and the year.

86. In 1996 this nineteen-year-old Brave outfielder became the youngest man to play in a LCS.

87. This lefty has pitched in the LCS for five teams. Name him and his clubs.

88. During the 1989 NLCS, these two opposing first basemen tore up mound deliveries with the victor hitting .650 and the loser .647.

89. He cracked three homers off Catfish Hunter in a losing cause in Game 3 of the 1978 ALCS.

90. This lefty reliever from Venezuela was the winning pitcher when the Blue Jays downed the Phillies 15–14 in Game 4 of the 1993 Series.

91. Which Hall of Famer started the first game of a World Series despite finishing three games under .500 during the regular season?

92. When was the first year the LCS switched to a best-of-seven format?

93. A year after being involved in the most infamous on-the-field tragedy, he started and won the first World Series game played by the Yankees.

94. Many remember the brawl between Pete Rose and Bud Harrelson in Game 3 of the 1973 NLCS. But can you recall the Reds' starter and loser whom the Mets drove from the mound in the second inning?

95. It was his shot that Willie Mays snagged while running with his back to the plate in the opening game of the 1954 Series.

96. This Tiger left fielder ended Game 1 of the 1968 Series when he was caught looking, giving Bob Gibson his 17th strikeout.

97. This Hall of Famer's career ended after the final game of the 1951 Series.

98. They not only lost a LCS after being up three games to one, but they turned the trick twice in World Series play.

99. The first pitcher to start a World Series game for Brooklyn was later elected to the Hall of Fame.

100. Although Grover Alexander saved the day when he fanned Tony Lazzeri with the bases loaded in the deciding game of the 1926 Series, it was this Hall of Famer who started and won the contest for the Cards.

101. During the period when the Braves boasted Maddux, Smoltz, Glavine, and Avery, it was this man who started Atlanta's first game in World Series play.

102. In 1947 this 5'7" lefty was the only Brooklyn hurler given as many as two starts in the seven-game Series against the Yanks.

103. This skipper was ejected from Game 6 of the 1996 Classic.

104. Name the team that swept its opponents in the LCS and then proceeded to do the same in the World Series.

105. Despite his record-tying 12 hits in the 1996 Series, his team fell to the Yanks.

106. In 1996 he became the first reliever to record a save in each of his team's four World Series victories.

107. The first closer to notch a save in each of his team's four LCS wins did it in 1988.

108. Johnny Antonelli allowed a leadoff homer to this Cleveland outfielder in Game 2 of the 1954 Series and then shut the Tribe down the rest of the way.

109. He went the free-agent route after winning 2 games for the Blue Jays during their 1992 clash with the Braves.

110. This southpaw started games in the LCS for Davey Johnson as a Red in 1995 and then as an Oriole the following year.

111. The two hurlers who squared off in Game 1 of the 1939 World Series had also been given the starting nod in that year's All-Star game.

112. Identify the Yankee reliever who lost Games 3, 4, and 6 in the 1981 Series.

113. In his only season of big league action, he was stationed at first for the 1941 Yanks and recorded more at-bats than any other player in the Series.

114. This Cardinal third baseman's two-run shot in the ninth gave the Redbirds the 1942 World Championship, handing the Bombers their first defeat in their last nine Series appearances.

115. He was the only man to play in all 44 World Series games between the Yankees and the Dodgers between 1941 and 1956.

116. Born in Poland, this Oriole reliever set the tone for the 1966 Series when he fanned 11 Dodgers in 6$^2/3$ innings of work.

117. Whitey Ford won his first World Series starting assignment when he downed this Phillie rookie in Game 4 to end the 1950 Classic.

118. The 1954 Indians' pitching staff was so deep that this Hall of Famer rode the bench during the Series despite a 13–3 regular season record.

119. Name the only player to connect for a four-bagger in the infamous 1919 Series.

120. When the Red Sox won 4 World Series between 1912 and 1918, which outfielder played in all 24 games?

121. When the Boston Braves won their only World Championship in 1914, which Hall of Fame second baseman batted .438 during the clash?

122. After dropping his first two starts to the Giants during the 1924 Series, this Hall of Famer redeemed himself by winning the deciding game in relief.

123. Name the two catchers who batted .533 and .529 respectively during the 1976 Series.

124. This Phillie shut out the Blue Jays in Game 5 of the 1993 Series after Toronto had scored 25 runs over the previous two contests.

125. Identify the Hall of Famer who ended his career at third base, batting .190 for the Giants in the 1936 Series.

126. The only player to pop 2 homers during the 1935 Series was this Cub outfielder who had connected just twice during the regular season.

127. Bound for Cooperstown, this man, who later gained fame at second base, served as the Giants hot cornerman in 1921, batting .300 in the Series.

128. In 1948 he started and lost the last World Series game played by the Boston Braves.

129. He dropped all three of his starting assignments for the White Sox in the 1919 Series.

130. Despite this Hall of Famer batting only .235 for Brooklyn in the 1941 Series, his figure topped all other Dodger regulars.

131. A .260 lifetime hitter, this Buc infielder rapped Baltimore for a .500 average during the 1979 Series.

132. Another scrappy infielder who rose to the occasion was this .257 career batter who compiled a .500 figure for the Yanks in the 1953 clash.

133. His .500 mark at the plate for Cleveland led all others in a losing cause during the 1954 Classic.

134. The last team to fail to homer during a Fall Classic was swept in their first Series appearance in thirty-five years.

135. Starting on only one day's rest, this Cub failed to retire one batter in his deciding-game loss to the Tigers in the 1945 Series.

136. This Bosox hurler accounted for their only run with a home run in a 2–1 loss to Bob Gibson in Game 1 of the 1967 Series.

137. Name the curveball artist who appeared in the LCS for Minnesota in 1970 and in 1987.

138. Never a strikeout leader, this Hall of Famer turned it up a notch in the ALCS when he fanned 12 Twins in Game 3 in 1970 and 12 A's in the opener of 1973.

139. Stationed at short, he led Murderers' Row and all other regulars on either team with a .500 average during the 1927 matchup.

140. In 1990 this Cincinnati third baseman batted .563 during the Series, the highest figure for any regular who failed to lead in batting average.

141. He topped the L.A. Dodgers in batting during the 1974, 1977, and 1981 Series.

142. Identify the only man to appear in all 30 World Series games played between 1960 and 1964.

143. They scored only 8 runs in a seven-game set that went to Cleveland.

144. His 38 games of World Series' action leads all other first basemen.

145. The last man to hit a World Series homer for the original Senators was this outfielder who also led the team in batting during the 1933 Series.

146. These two men, later teammates on the first Yankee penant-winning team, accounted for all 4 wins in the Red Sox triumph over the Cubs in 1918.

147. Name the Redbird southpaw who won the clincher in the 1944 Series, jumped to the Mexican League in 1946, and was suspended by Major League Baseball for two years.

148. Only one man started against Sandy Koufax three times in one World Series. Name this fellow southpaw.

149. Michael was the given name of this man who played all 7 games at third for the Tigers in 1940 and for the Red Sox in 1946.

150. His tenth and final World Series appearance came as a member of the Red Sox in 1967.

151. This regular Tiger infielder batted .069 in the 1934 Series, then dropped to .050 in the following year's Series.

152. Which Hall of Fame spitballer pitched in World Series play for Brooklyn, the Cardinals, and the Cubs?

153. He pitched twice in relief for the L.A. Dodgers in 1981 before starting 8 World Series games in the A.L.

154. In Game 6 of the 1909 Classic, Detroit downed this Hall of Famer in the only World Series start of his career.

155. Al Simmons collected his last World Series hit for this N.L. team, which was swept by the Yanks in 1939.

156. This lefty picked up the first World Series win in Mets' history.

157. Who started and lost for the Dodgers when Don Larsen pitched his perfect game in 1956?

158. In 1910 the Philadelphia A's used only two pitchers to down the Cubs. Name this tandem.

159. This Yankee became the first rookie to power 3 homers in one series in 1939.

160. In 1957 he hit the first World Series homer by a player representing a team from Milwaukee.

CHAPTER THIRTEEN
All-Star Games

1. Which Yankee hurler started the first three All-Star games ever played?
2. Despite losing a league-leading 20 games, this Phillie lefty got the win in the 1944 contest.
3. The last time a now-defunct team hosted an All-Star game Willie McCovey clocked two homers to carry the N.L. to a 9–3 victory. What was the year, the city, and the name of the ballpark?
4. He was only nineteen years old when he pitched in the 1984 game.
5. Six players, three from each league, connected for homers in the 1971 matchup. All were later elected to the Hall of Fame.
6. Who received the starting nod in a record-tying 5 games during the 1950s?
7. Who are the only father and son to hit four-baggers in All-Star play?

8. This team, whose ballpark hosted the first midsummer classic in 1933, had to wait until 1995 for one of its players to hit an All-Star homer. Name the team and its star slugger.

9. After starting the 1980 game, this N.L. pitcher appeared in just one more regular season game before suffering a career-ending stroke.

10. Name the pitcher who appeared for the Phillies in the 1995 clash and failed to win another game the rest of the season.

11. Here's a guy who went from riches to rags. Just three years after starting the 1990 game with Cincinnati, his career had plummeted so far that he paced the Florida Marlins in losses during their inaugural season.

12. The only man to be chosen in the starting lineup who wore a first-year expansion team's uniform celebrated with a two-run homer in the opening frame.

13. In 1975 these two Dodgers became the only teammates to hit back-to-back homers.

14. In Oakland in 1987, his two-out triple in the top of the thirteenth drove in the only two runs of the game.

15. Which All-Star starter retired with only 16 career wins?

16. The loser for the A.L. in the 1995 All-Star game missed all of the 1996 season due to shoulder problems.

17. Of all the players who broke in since the inception of the All-Star game in 1933, this catcher played the most seasons without being chosen as a starter or a reserve.

18. This pitcher once dropped 27 decisions yet started two consecutive All-Star games later in his career.

19. Although Denny McLain and Bob Gibson won their leagues' Cy Young unanimously in 1968, neither started that year's midsummer classic. Which pair received the starting nods that year?

20. The first position player to appear in All-Star games in both leagues achieved the honor when he pinch-hit as a Yankee in the 1953 contest.

CHAPTER FOURTEEN

All-American Girls Professional Baseball League

1. Name the two Midwest states that operated throughout the AAGPL's run from 1943 to 1954.
2. After clobbering over 500 homers in the majors, he became a manager in the league.
3. Elected to the Hall in 1961, he not only managed a team but served as league president.
4. The team from a city currently represented in the A.L. won the league championship in the team's only year of existence. Name the city.
5. A perusal of the rule changes indicate a growing respect for the women's athletic ability. However, what was the original distance between home and the mound?

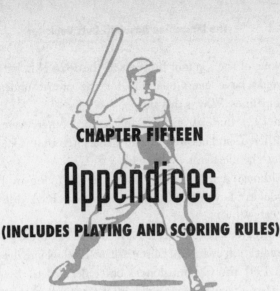

CHAPTER FIFTEEN
Appendices
(INCLUDES PLAYING AND SCORING RULES)

1. A National League fan during the 1870s rarely saw a pitcher walk more than one batter per game. Great control you say? Actually this edict was in effect.
2. Eleven men batted over .400 during the 1887 season because of what significant rule change revoked after the season?
3. Many baseball historians have questioned the methods of statistical comparison across eras. Particularly in question are analyses made prior to this design change in 1893 which reflects the game today. What was this crucial adjustment?
4. An examination of seasonal stolen-base totals beginning in the late 1880s through much of the 1890s reveals several players topping 100. What rule inflated players' totals during this period?
5. Prior to 1920 forty players, including Babe Ruth, whacked balls out of the park to win games for their teams yet were denied homers because of a rule that has since been eliminated. Describe it.

6. None of the top four finishers in the 1926 N.L. batting race would have even qualified for the crown under today's guidelines. Why is this so?

7. In 1921 Burleigh Grimes and sixteen others were "grand-fathered" and allowed to throw this pitch that would henceforth be illegal for anyone else.

8. Although Greg Maddux won the Cy Young in 1993, he wouldn't have officially qualified for the ERA title prior to 1951. Why?

9. Keith Hernandez collected a record 129 of these prior to its eradication as an official statistic in 1989. Name the stat.

10. In 1991 the Commissioner's office decided to disallow no-hitters previously accepted in the records that fell under three criteria. Which types of no-hitters would no longer be officially recognized?

CHAPTER SIXTEEN

Answers

CHAPTER ONE: HISTORY OF BASEBALL

1. Alexander Cartwright
2. Henry Chadwick
3. King Kelly
4. Monte Ward
5. Western League
6. Rube Foster
7. 1939
8. Danny Gardella
9. Nolan Ryan
10. Bud Selig

CHAPTER TWO: SPECIAL ACHIEVEMENTS

1. Denny McLain
2. Bobby Richardson
3. Donn Clendenon
4. Nellie Fox
5. Lou Pinella (Baltimore and Cleveland)
6. Sandy Alomar Jr.
7. Lou Whitaker
8. Minnie Minoso, left field; Willie Mays, center field; Al Kaline, right field
9. Ted Williams
10. Jackie Robinson
11. Joe Charboneau
12. Steve Stone
13. Juan Marichal
14. Jim Lefebvre, Joe Morgan
15. Buck Ewing
16. Tony LaRussa
17. Luis Aparico
18. Jay Bell
19. Bob Boone
20. Jim Kaat
21. Aurelio Rodriguez
22. Lou Gehrig, Mickey Cochrane
23. Gus Suhr

24. Dick Fowler
25. Ramon and Pedro Martinez
26. Maury Wills
27. LaMarr Hoyt
28. Steve Bedrosian
29. Steve Busby
30. Bob Turley
31. George Bell
32. Weldon Henley
33. Bart Giamatti
34. Jim Maloney
35. Mark Fidrych
36. Dwight Gooden
37. Thurman Munson, Carl Morton
38. Lou Pinella, Alvin Dark
39. Vince Coleman
40. Bob Grim
41. Jose Canseco (Ozzie Canseco)
42. Tony Oliva
43. Fred Lynn
44. Fernando Valenzuela
45. Herb Score, John Montefusco, Hideo Nomo
46. Albie Pearson
47. Jack Sanford
48. Ken Hubbs
49. Jeff Bagwell, Frank Thomas
50. Denny McLain, Bill Freehan
51. Billy Williams
52. Sandy Koufax
53. Joe Torre
54. Kenny Rogers
55. Al Kaline
56. Catfish Hunter
57. Mike Witt
58. Joe Cowley
59. Tony Mullane, Guy Hecker
60. Bill Stoneman
61. Addie Joss
62. Hugh "One Arm" Daily
63. Dave Stewart, Fernando Valenzuela
64. Ted Breitenstein
65. Monte Ward
66. Pat Listach
67. All-Star Game
68. Rick Sutcliffe
69. Bo Belinsky
70. Mark McGwire
71. Andres Galarraga
72. Walter Johnson
73. 75 percent
74. Roberto Clemente
75. Ernie Banks
76. Lee MacPhail
77. Kenesaw Mountain Landis
78. Bob Gibson
79. Maury Wills
80. Mort and Walker Cooper
81. Al Dark
82. Bob Elliott
83. Jeff Burroughs
84. Willie Stargell
85. Barry Bonds
86. Hank Greenberg, Robin Yount
87. Sherm Lollar
88. Bob Keegan
89. Jim Bunning
90. Ken Holtzman, Rick Wise
91. Ralph Kiner
92. Lou Gehrig
93. Hank Greenberg
94. Johnny Mize
95. Al Cowens
96. Greg Luzinski
97. Billy Williams
98. Tommy Davis
99. Jim Lonborg
100. Chipper Jones
101. Rick Reuschel
102. Mark Langston, Al Davis

103. Frank Malzone
104. Charles Johnson
105. Pete Rose
106. Jim Kaat, Earl Battey
107. Mark Davis
108. Larry Jansen
109. Tom Browning
110. Willie McCovey, Orlando Cepeda
111. Red Ames
112. Dennis Eckersley
113. Pittsburgh Pirates
114. Dean Chance
115. Willie Hernandez
116. Tom Seaver
117. Dick Groat
118. Kevin Seitzer
119. Johnny Vander Meer
120. Nap Lajoie
121. Joe Medwick
122. Jimmie Foxx and Chuck Klein in Philadelphia
123. Mickey Mantle
124. Ty Cobb
125. William Eckert
126. Dick Burns
127. Yankees, Hoyt Wilhelm
128. Astros, Mets
129. Everett Scott
130. Steve Carlton
131. Larry Corcoran
132. Jim Spencer
133. Warren Spahn
134. Cincinnati Reds
135. Jackie Robinson
136. Ken Johnson
137. Bret Saberhagen
138. Mike McCormick (San Francisco), David Cone (Kansas City)
139. Ken Griffey Sr. and Ken Griffey Jr.

140. Bobby Richardson
141. Ray Knight
142. Cy Young
143. Johnny Bench, Carlton Fisk
144. Jocko Conlon
145. Lou Gehrig
146. Ford Frick
147. Ned Hanlon
148. Mickey Mantle, Whitey Ford
149. Bowie Kuhn
150. Hugh Jennings
151. Connie Mack, John McGraw, George Wright
152. Nolan Ryan
153. Phil Niekro
154. Eddie Plank and Rube Waddell
155. Nellie Fox and Luis Aparicio, White Sox
156. Ross Youngs
157. Cesar Cedeno
158. Ruben Amaro and Bobby Wine
159. Tommie Agee, 1970
160. Clete and Ken Boyer
161. Al Bumbry
162. Harry Byrd
163. Gary Peters
164. Kent Mercker
165. Gary Pettis
166. Garry Maddox
167. Roberto Clemente
168. Tim Wallach
169. Curt Flood
170. Doug Drabek
171. Tony Armas
172. Cecil Fielder—tied for homer lead in 1991 with Jose Canseco
173. Mickey Lolich
174. Hideo Nomo
175. Randy Johnson
176. Don Newcombe
177. Bob Horner
178. Rod Carew

179. Tommie Agee
180. Tom Tresh
181. Tommy Helms
182. Gil McDougald
183. Stan Bahnsen
184. Harvey Kuenn
185. Chris Sabo
186. Benito Santiago
187. Jim Gilliam
188. Ron Kittle
189. Billy Williams
190. Dick Allen
191. Joe Black
192. Don Schwall
193. Rick Sutcliffe
194. Walt Dropo
195. Willie Mays
196. Bob Moose
197. Dick Bosman
198. Jim Bunning
199. Cliff Chambers
200. Mike Scott
201. Mel Parnell
202. Bob Lemon
203. Wilson Alvarez
204. Ed Cicotte
205. Dusty Baker
206. John Wetteland
207. Don Larsen
208. Larry Sherry
209. Andre Dawson
210. Dave Righetti
211. Fred Lynn
212. Bill Virdon
213. Frank Robinson
214. Sparky Anderson
215. Buck Showalter
216. Bob Forsch
217. Virgil Trucks
218. Buck Rodgers
219. Jack Kralick
220. Len Barker

221. Carl Erskine
222. Bob Gibson
223. Warren Spahn
224. Cincinnati Reds
225. George Foster, George Mogridge
226. Dale Murphy
227. Bake McBride
228. Tony Kubek
229. Todd Worrell
230. Walt Weiss
231. Steve Howe
232. Darryl Strawberry
233. Dave Justice
234. Ozzie Guillen
235. Dave Stieb
236. Eddie Yost
237. George Mullin
238. Bob Feller
239. Allie Reynolds
240. Bill Dineen
241. Frank Smith
242. Bobo Holloman
243. Charlie Robertson
244. Hod Eller
245. Rube Marquard
246. Sam Jones
247. Earl Williams
248. Luis Aparicio
249. Mike Piazza
250. Jim Landis
251. Ken Holtzman
252. Sal Maglie
253. Steve Barber, Stu Miller
254. Jon Matlack
255. Gregg Olson
256. Carlton Fisk
257. Pud Galvin
258. Rex Barney
259. Willie Davis
260. Rick Miller
261. Raul Mondesi

262. Babe Ruth
263. Mike Warren
264. Ted Lyons

265. Mike Norris
266. Nolan Ryan

CHAPTER THREE: ALL-TIME LEADERS

1. Nolan Ryan
2. Eddie Murray
3. Ozzie Smith
4. Don Money
5. Mike Boddicker
6. Steve Garvey
7. Dwayne Murphy
8. Buddy Rosar
9. Dom DiMaggio
10. Stuffy McInnis
11. Bill Buckner
12. Happy Felsch
13. Frankie Frisch
14. Taylor Douthit
15. Johnny Edwards
16. Jiggs Donahue
17. Denny Lyons
18. Rabbit Maranville
19. Dave Bancroft
20. Bid McPhee
21. Graig Nettles
22. Tony Fernandez
23. Eddie Collins
24. Rusty Staub
25. Sam Crawford
26. Stan Musial
27. Roberto Clemente
28. Tommy Corcoran
29. Fred Tenney
30. Chuck Klein
31. Jimmy Williams, Tommy Leach
32. Ferris Fain
33. Jack Morris
34. Willie Mays
35. Gary Carter
36. Bill Dahlen

37. Phil Niekro
38. Ray Schalk
39. Cy Young
40. Dave Cash
41. John Vander Wal
42. Jake Beckley
43. Goose Goslin
44. Eddie Yost
45. Grover Alexander
46. Roger Connor
47. Vic Willis
48. Pud Galvin
49. George Foster
50. Old Hoss Radbourn
51. Pete Incaviglia
52. Wayne Granger
53. Lefty O'Doul
54. Rob Deer
55. Sam Thompson
56. Smoky Burgess
57. Cannonball Ed Morris
58. Billy Herman
59. Dave Nicholson
60. Gene Garber
61. Al Kaline
62. Bob Gibson
63. Christy Mathewson
64. Catfish Hunter
65. Art Nehf, Waite Hoyt
66. Red Lucas
67. Ty Cobb
68. Orel Hershiser
69. Jerry Reuss
70. Steve Carlton
71. Dave Stewart
72. Steve Garvey

73. George Brett
74. Reggie Jackson
75. Yogi Berra
76. Paul Molitor
77. Frankie Frisch
78. Hank Greenberg
79. Nolan Ryan
80. Frank Robinson
81. Lou Brock
82. Ted Breitenstein
83. Lou Gehrig, Chuck Klein
84. Bobby Bonds
85. Willie Wilson, Juan Samuel
86. Stan Musial
87. Hi Bithorn
88. Harmon Killebrew
89. Paul Waner
90. Dave Kingman
91. Mel Ott (Rogers Hornsby had 999 in the N.L.)
92. Runs Scored, 2174
93. Rickey Henderson
94. Joe Morgan
95. Lou Brock
96. Babe Ruth, .342
97. Ted Williams
98. Reggie Jackson
99. Rollie Fingers
100. Lee Smith
101. Bobby Thigpen
102. Roy Face
103. Sparky Lyle
104. Fergie Jenkins
105. Bruce Sutter
106. Joe Judge
107. Al Kaline
108. Darrell Evans
109. Max Carey
110. Cy Young
111. Don Sutton
112. Joe Morgan

113. Tim Keefe
114. Eddie Plank
115. Bob Friend
116. George Uhle
117. Steve Carlton
118. Mel Harder
119. Ty Cobb
120. Eddie Plank
121. Bert Blyleven
122. Phil Niekro
123. Robin Roberts
124. Enos Slaughter
125. Tommy Davis
126. Mickey Mantle
127. Hoyt Wilhelm
128. Honus Wagner
129. Carl Yastrzemski
130. Frank Robinson
131. Jimmie Foxx: Philadelphia A's and Boston Red Sox
132. Ty Cobb
133. Wade Boggs
134. Stan Musial
135. Tris Speaker
136. Don Sutton
137. Kiki Cuyler
138. Ralph Kiner
139. Bert Blyleven
140. Dave Winfield, Paul Molitor
141. Jimmie Foxx
142. Ty Cobb, Tris Speaker
143. Willie McCovey
144. Vince Coleman
145. Carl Yastrzemski
146. Nolan Ryan
147. Jake Beckley
148. Eppa Rixey
149. Hugh Casey
150. Barry Bonds
151. Billy Williams

CHAPTER FOUR: LIFETIME MAJOR LEAGUE TEAM ROSTERS

1. Boston Braves
2. Zack Wheat
3. Paul Hines
4. Players' League
5. Ed Bressoud
6. Cleveland Indians
7. St. Louis Browns
8. Alex Trevino
9. Blue Jays
10. Chicago Cubs
11. Columbus and Toledo
12. Chicago
13. Lonnie Frey
14. Doc Crandall
15. Gene Woodling
16. Jack Harper
17. Ed Mathews
18. Diego Segui
19. Oakland A's
20. Baltimore

CHAPTER FIVE: THE TEAMS AND THEIR PLAYERS

1. Ralph Garr
2. Gary Sheffield
3. Willie Randolph
4. Hal Morris
5. Wid Conroy
6. Willie Keeler, Joe Kelley, Steve Brodie
7. Old Hoss Radbourn, Dan Brouthers, King Kelly
8. Del Pratt
9. Andre Rodgers
10. Vern Stephens
11. Gorman Thomas
12. Clyde Wright
13. Colorado Rockies
14. Dave Concepcion
15. Connie Mack
16. Mike Donlin
17. 1984 Padres: Eric Show and Alan Wiggins
18. Milwaukee Brewers
19. 1962
20. Fred Pfeffer
21. Darrell Brandon
22. Len Dykstra
23. 1924 White Sox
24. Red Sox: Jimmie Foxx, first base; Bobby Doerr, second base; Joe Cronin, shortstop; Jim Tabor, third base.
25. 1948, Chicago Cubs and White Sox
26. Blue Jays
27. Merv Rettenmund
28. 1941 Yankees: Tommy Henrich, Joe DiMaggio, Charlie Keller
29. Twins: Bob Allison, Jimmie Hall, Harmon Killebrew
30. Jim Devlin
31. Case Patten
32. Cleveland and Chicago
33. Hal Chase
34. Tigers: Charlie Gehringer, Gee Walker
35. Gus Zernial
36. Eddie Moore
37. Bill Caudill
38. Larry Walker, Vinny Castilla, Andres Galarraga, Dante Bichette
39. Phillies, Robin Roberts, Richie Ashburn

40. Ed Delahanty
41. John Olerud, Paul Molitor, Roberto Alomar
42. Matty and Felipe Alou
43. Graeme Lloyd, Dave Nilsson
44. Ty Cobb, Sam Crawford
45. 1995 Cleveland Indians
46. Wally Bunker
47. Bobo Newsom
48. Chuck Hinton
49. Bob Porterfield
50. Jim Finigan
51. Rusty Staub
52. Wee Willie Keeler
53. Urban Shocker
54. George Stone
55. Fergie Jenkins
56. Earl Averill
57. Tony Oliva
58. Charlie Root
59. Zack Wheat
60. Ed Charles
61. Willie McCovey, 469
62. Dick Rudolph
63. Ed Brinkman
64. Tony Fernandez
65. Felix Millan
66. Jeff Conine
67. Jack Powell
68. Joe Nuxhall
69. Fred Kendall
70. Milwaukee Brewers
71. San Diego Padres
72. Ewell Blackwell
73. White Sox: Luke Appling
74. Wilbert Robinson, Roger Bresnahan
75. Harry Simpson
76. Washington: Roy Sievers
77. Cincinnati Reds
78. Pud Galvin
79. St. Louis Browns

80. Darold Knowles
81. Danny Cox, Greg Mathews, Bob Forsch
82. Alvaro Espinoza
83. New York Mets, .242
84. Ken Harrelson
85. Harry Heilmann, Ty Cobb, Heinie Manush
86. Milwaukee, 1965: Hank Aaron, Eddie Mathews, Mack Jones, Joe Torre, Felipe Alou, Gene Oliver
87. Boston
88. Willie Wilson
89. Lady Baldwin
90. Todd Worrell
91. Enzo Hernandez
92. Chicago, Detroit, Boston, Cleveland
93. Indianapolis, 1914
94. N.Y. Giants, 1915
95. Hartford Dark Blues
96. L.A. Dodgers, 1959
97. St. Louis Maroons
98. Chicago Cubs, 1938
99. Harmon Killebrew
100. Willie McCovey
101. Aaron Ward, Everett Scott
102. Bryan Rekar
103. Ralph Garr
104. Willie Mays
105. Bobby Bonds
106. Gary Sheffield
107. Alex Johnson
108. Lance Johnson
109. George Bell
110. Johnny Antonelli
111. Grover Alexander, 1917
112. Dwight Gooden
113. 1975 Cincinnati Reds
114. Baltimore Orioles
115. Tony Cloninger

116. Jim Colborn
117. Larry Dierker
118. Paul Splittorff
119. John Burkett, Bill Swift
120. Sam Rice, Tris Speaker, Goose Goslin
121. Buzz Capra
122. Hoyt Wilhelm
123. Allan Anderson
124. Ed Reulbach
125. Dave Davenport
126. Dan Brouthers
127. California Angels, 1973: Nolan Ryan, Bill Singer
128. Phillies, 1914: Grover Alexander, Erskine Mayer
129. Jesse Burkett
130. Willie Upshaw
131. Pete Rose, Tony Perez, Buddy Bell, Dave Concepcion, Cesar Cedeno
132. Bob Tillman
133. Detroit Tigers
134. Pittsburgh Pirates
135. Yankees 1947-58
136. L.A. Angels, 1962
137. George Scott, Ben Ogilvie, Gorman Thomas
138. Phil Bradley
139. Travis Fryman
140. L.A. Dodgers
141. Houston Colt .45's
142. L.A. Dodgers
143. Cleveland: Jerry Kindall and Woodie Held
144. Dan Schatzeder
145. Earl Battey
146. Tom Parsons
147. Skeeter Webb
148. Darrell Evans, Davey Johnson, Hank Aaron
149. Jack Morris, 1992
150. Ray Mueller
151. Randy Lerch
152. Bob Boyd
153. Bob Bailor
154. Houston Astros' Jose Cruz
155. Jose, Hector, and Tommy Cruz
156. Chicago White Sox, 1918
157. Turner Barber
158. Louisville
159. Ross Grimsley
160. Bill Freehan
161. Babe Ruth
162. Dick Selma
163. Kevin Elster
164. Tom Timmerman
165. Garland Braxton
166. Wilcy Moore, Waite Hoyt, Urban Shocker
167. Houston Astros
168. New York Highlanders, now Yankees
169. Jake Daubert
170. Sam Crawford
171. Vida Blue
172. Vic Raschi
173. Roscoe Miller
174. Bill Bernhard
175. Tom Seaver
176. Sammy Vick
177. Carmen Hill
178. Slim Love
179. Dave McNally
180. Jeff Conine
181. Otis Nixon
182. Alex Rodriguez
183. Don Mattingly
184. Robin Yount
185. Bill Mazeroski
186. George Brett
187. Cal Ripken
188. Pie Traynor
189. Cap Anson

190. Pee Wee Reese
191. Eddie Mathews
192. Brooks Robinson
193. Hank Greenberg
194. Honus Wagner
195. Lou Brock
196. Willie Mays
197. Lou Gehrig
198. Bill Terry
199. Bobby Doerr
200. Charlie Gehringer
201. Ernie Banks
202. Luke Appling
203. Dave Winfield
204. Carlton Fisk
205. St. Louis Cardinals
206. Ken Griffey, Jr.
207. Gary Carter
208. Ryne Sandberg
209. Jeff Bagwell
210. Tony Lazzeri
211. Reggie Jackson
212. Al Kaline
213. Mark McGwire
214. Pete Rose
215. George Van Haltren
216. Buddy Bell
217. Ellis Burks, 1996
218. Craig Biggio
219. Damaso Garcia
220. Willie Davis
221. Bert Campaneris
222. Davey Lopes
223. Dom DiMaggio
224. Clyde Milan
225. Max Carey
226. Eddie and Johnny O'Brien
227. Jimmie Foxx, Red Sox, 1938
228. Tim Crews, Steve Olin
229. Cliff Young
230. Jim Bottomley

231. George Sisler
232. Rod Carew
233. Jackie Robinson
234. Jim Lemon
235. Vic Wertz
236. Camilo Pascual
237. L.A. Dodgers, 1965
238. Pat Malone
239. Warren Spahn
240. Quilvio Veras
241. Stan Coveleski
242. Ken Caminiti
243. Joe Jackson
244. Al Simmons
245. Zack Wheat
246. Johnny Mize
247. Ross Youngs
248. Jim Bottomley
249. Danny Thompson
250. Juan Guzman
251. Bob Johnson
252. Johnny Lindell
253. Arky Vaughn
254. Frankie Crosetti
255. Bill Dickey
256. Cass Michaels
257. Joe Tinker
258. Bobby Veach
259. Jorge Orta
260. Fred Lindstrom
261. Ivy Olson
262. Rick Monday
263. Philadelphia A's
264. Ron Fairly
265. Chuck Klein
266. George Sisler
267. Denny McLain
268. Ollie Brown
269. Rich Hand
270. Greg Luzinski
271. Charlie Hayes

CHAPTER SIX: HOME/ROAD PERFORMANCE

1. New York Giants
2. Red Sox
3. 1906 Cubs
4. Philadelphia A's
5. Browns, 1944
6. 1995 Braves and Indians
7. Milwaukee Brewers
8. Tigers, 1984
9. Red Sox
10. Cleveland Indians
11. Rockies, 1995
12. 1984
13. Yankees, 1950
14. Leo Durocher: Giants, 1951; Cubs, 1969
15. Brooklyn Dodgers
16. 1927 Pirates
17. Yankees, 1923
18. Cardinals, 1928
19. Philadelphia A's, 1916
20. Boston Braves
21. 1962 Mets
22. Boston Braves, 1911
23. Reds
24. N.Y. Giants
25. Yankees, 1933

26. Philadelphia A's
27. Yankees
28. Phillies, 1930
29. Baltimore Orioles
30. Expos
31. Philadelphia A's
32. 1918
33. Pirates, 1952
34. Browns
35. Phillies, 1942
36. Milwaukee Braves
37. Indianapolis
38. Indians, 1917
39. L.A. Angels, 1961
40. Washington
41. Baltimore Orioles
42. Oakland A's
43. Cincinnati Reds
44. Philadelphia A's, 1931
45. Red Sox
46. Detroit
47. Cubs
48. N.Y. Giants
49. Washington Senators
50. Washington Senators

CHAPTER SEVEN: MANAGERS

1. Third
2. Leo Durocher
3. Fred Haney
4. Dusty Baker
5. Frank Chance
6. Connie Mack
7. Bill McKechnie
8. Joe McCarthy
9. Steve O'Neill
10. Jimmy Dykes
11. George Stallings

12. Ralph Houk
13. Gene Mauch
14. Herman Franks
15. Jack Barry, 90 in 1917 with the Red Sox
16. Walt Alston
17. Bill McGunnigle, Brooklyn
18. Buck Showalter
19. Frank Selee, Boston, 1898
20. Chuck Dressen
21. Clark Griffith

22. Kid Nichols, Cardinals, 1904
23. Hank Bauer
24. Jim McAleer
25. Billy Meyer
26. John McNamara
27. Preston Gomez
28. Cookie Lavagetto
29. Joe Gordon
30. Tony LaRussa
31. Tom Kelly
32. Mel Ott, 1942
33. Dave Bristol
34. Danny Ozark
35. Jim Lemon
36. Marcel and Rene Lachemann
37. Bobby Mattick
38. Frank Robinson
39. Patsy Tebeau
40. Bob Lemon
41. Doc Prothro
42. Roy Hartsfield
43. Kaiser Wilhelm
44. Jack Chapman
45. Pie Traynor, George Gibson
46. Bill Rigney
47. Bill Carrigan
48. Ben Chapman
49. Fred Clarke
50. Hughie Jennings
51. Billy Barnie
52. Joe Cantillon
53. Red Schoendienst
54. Cito Gaston
55. Dick Howser
56. Del Crandall
57. Pat Corrales
58. Bruce Bochy
59. Dick Williams
60. Miller Huggins
61. Lou Boudreau and Satchel Paige

62. George and Dick Sisler
63. Art Irwin
64. Bill Plummer
65. Sparky Anderson
66. Larry Doby
67. Bob Coleman
68. Bobby Bragan
69. Zack Taylor
70. Felipe Alou, 1994
71. Johnny Keane
72. Bobby Winkles
73. Jack McKeon
74. Cap Anson
75. Cal Ripken, Sr.
76. Tommy Lasorda
77. Roger Craig
78. Tommy Holmes
79. Yogi Berra
80. Whitey Herzog
81. Ted Williams
82. Harry Craft
83. Al Spalding
84. Harry Walker
85. Jim Lefebvre
86. Jack O'Connor
87. Earl Weaver
88. John McGraw
89. Ned Hanlon
90. Jim Marshall
91. Burt Shotton
92. Billy Martin
93. Jim Leyland
94. Billy Southworth
95. Eddie Dyer
96. Al Dark
97. Joe McCarthy
98. Harry Wright
99. Gabby Hartnett
100. Frank Robinson

CHAPTER EIGHT: PLAYERS AND PITCHERS

1. Stan Musial
2. Mike Schmidt
3. Ed Walsh
4. Lou Whitaker and Alan Trammell
5. Beau Bell, Sammy West, Joe Vosmik
6. Fergie Jenkins
7. J. R. Richard
8. Reggie Jackson, Tony Perez
9. Luke Easter
10. Frank Howard
11. Mark Eichhorn
12. Buddy Bell
13. Jimmy Wynn
14. Eddie Mathews
15. Mike Parrott
16. Al Oliver
17. Bill Campbell
18. Nap Lajoie
19. Al Simmons, 1929-30
20. Bill Dineen
21. Ron Gant
22. Russ Ford, Cy Falkenberg
23. Jesse Burkett
24. Turk Farrell
25. Bob Elliott and Marty Marion
26. Ken Singleton
27. Joe Hauser
28. Miguel Dilone
29. Dummy Hoy
30. Allen Sothoron
31. Bobby Shantz
32. Kid Gleason
33. Irish Meusel
34. Joe Coleman
35. Ken Harrelson
36. Milt Pappas
37. Gary Nolan
38. Ed McKean and Joe Cronin
39. Joe Medwick and Wade Boggs
40. Denis Menke
41. Ted Lyons
42. Jack Quinn
43. Bucky Walters
44. Satchel Paige
45. Harlond Clift
46. Goose Goslin
47. Grover Alexander
48. Hank Aaron, 1973
49. Dave Righetti
50. Jim Levey
51. Wally Moses
52. Ken Phelps
53. John Clarkson
54. Don Sutton
55. Ted Williams and Dave Robertson
56. Gaylord Perry and Nolan Ryan
57. Rollie Fingers, 114
58. Dick Barrett, 1945 Phillies
59. Dennis Eckersley
60. Bob Stanley
61. Willie Wilson
62. Charlie Hough
63. Luis Olmo
64. Curt Davis
65. Dave Collins
66. Sam McDowell
67. Roy Smalley Jr. and Roy Smalley III
68. Fred Dunlap
69. Bill Nicholson
70. Jeff Russell
71. Manny Lee
72. Jeff Reardon and Brian Harvey
73. Bert Campaneris
74. Gavvy Cravath
75. Dave Orr
76. Mike Torrez

77. Rick Wise
78. Kent Tekulve
79. Tom Henke
80. Goose Gossage
81. Matty Alou
82. Don Drysdale
83. Carlos Baerga
84. Early Wynn
85. George Davis
86. Herman Long
87. Howard Ehmke
88. Wilbur Cooper
89. Pinky Whitney
90. Sherry Magee
91. Albert Belle
92. Cecil Fielder
93. Dizzy Dean
94. Jack Clements
95. Paul and Lloyd Waner
96. Eddie Murray and Ozzie Smith
97. Mel Ott
98. Joe Magrane
99. Kirby Puckett
100. Don Sutton
101. Harry Davis
102. Bobby Thigpen
103. Mark Koenig
104. Jack Graham
105. Bob Feller
106. Jimmie Foxx
107. Greg Vaughn
108. Pete Rose
109. Paul Molitor
110. Willie Keeler
111. Larry Bowa
112. Eppa Rixey
113. Clay Kirby
114. Tommy Holmes
115. Amos Rusie
116. Dan Ford
117. Pat Seerey

118. Vince DiMaggio, Pancho Herrera, and Jim Lemon
119. Ron Fairly
120. Lou Gehrig
121. Fred Luderus
122. Milt Gaston
123. Joe DiMaggio
124. Matt Kilroy
125. Lou Brock
126. Edgar Martinez
127. Lefty Grove
128. Tom Seaton
129. Jim Gentile
130. Max Bishop
131. Ben Oglivie
132. Doc White (Eddie Cicotte also had these numbers but he is blacklisted.)
133. Tom Zachary
134. Deacon White
135. Ted Williams
136. Tris Speaker
137. Jack Coffey
138. Andres Galarraga
139. Bobby Avila
140. Dave Winfield
141. Waite Hoyt
142. Earl Averill
143. Rudy York
144. Cy Young
145. Eddie Collins
146. Ripper Collins
147. Lou Jackson
148. Roy Cullenbine
149. Catfish Hunter
150. Harmon Killebrew
151. Carlton Fisk
152. Tommy Harper, Chuck Carr
153. Bill Dickey
154. Brian Harper
155. Juan Beniquez

156. Nick Cullop
157. Ken Williams
158. Ken Boyer
159. Fred Lynn
160. Dean Chance
161. Willie Mays
162. John Tudor
163. Chick Fraser
164. Clark Griffith
165. Ivan Rodriguez
166. Dave Magadan, Lou Pinella
167. Beau Bell
168. Jerry Reuss
169. Jim Tobin
170. Eddie Ainsmith, 48
171. Nap Reyes
172. Luke Appling
173. Harold Baines
174. Hank Aaron
175. Wes Covington
176. Harold Reynolds
177. Charlie Gehringer
178. Ned Garver
179. Tommy Herr
180. Don Buford
181. Jack Glasscock
182. Mike Jorgensen
183. Bob Saverine
184. Herb Washington
185. Larry Lintz
186. Bert Cunningham
187. Mike Bielecki
188. Snuffy Stirnweiss
189. Hank Borowy
190. Sal Maglie
191. Joe Jackson
192. Garry Templeton
193. Dizzy and Paul Dean
194. Todd Stottlemyre, son of Mel
195. Carlos, Melido, and Pascual
Perez

196. Cloyd, Clete, and Ken Boyer
197. Don Mattingly
198. Roger Craig
199. Eddie Mathews
200. Gary Peters
201. Sadowski
202. Sparky Adams
203. Jim Bunning
204. John Wathan
205. Al Simmons
206. Tip O'Neill
207. Larry Andersen
208. Rogers Hornsby
209. Hank Aaron
210. Ted Kluszewski
211. Johnny Mize
212. George Brett
213. Darrell Evans
214. Ivan Rodriguez
215. Tommy John
216. Nap Lajoie
217. Dale Mitchell
218. Stan Musial
219. Hank Greenberg
220. Dennis Martinez
221. Jim Palmer
222. Robin Roberts
223. Dick Radatz
224. Bob Elliott
225. Lou Brock
226. Howard Johnson
227. Ralph Kiner
228. Mike Moore
229. Nolan Ryan
230. Wade Boggs
231. Lloyd Waner
232. Bob Hazle
233. Duke Snider
234. Cal Ripken
235. Freddie Fitzsimmons
236. Deacon McGuire

237. Jim Merritt
238. Del Ennis
239. Carl Scheib
240. Ed Delahanty
241. Rip Sewell
242. Greg Maddux
243. Ron LeFlore
244. Ron Bryant
245. Bill Melton
246. Dick Allen
247. Lou Gehrig
248. Sam Rice
249. Willis Hudlin
250. Tom Seaver
251. Vern Stephens
252. Rick Honeycutt
253. Al Simmons
254. Zack Wheat
255. Eddie Stanky, 2B; Eddie Joost, SS; Eddie Yost, 3B
256. Hughie Jennnings
257. Babe Ruth 118 in 1916
258. Bob Gibson
259. Christy Mathewson, Joe McGinnity
260. Andres Galarraga
261. Tony Gwynn
262. Reggie Jackson
263. Tommy Bond
264. Mel Ott
265. Fred Lindstrom
266. Dick Stuart
267. Jackie Robinson
268. Bill Buckner
269. Rogers Hornsby, George Sisler; 1922, St. Louis
270. Joe Dugan
271. Richie Ashburn
272. John Franco
273. Dave Giusti
274. Robin Roberts
275. Bob Johnson

276. Tony Perez
277. Dave Kingman
278. Tommy John
279. Luis Tiant
280. Matty Alou
281. Kirby Puckett
282. Hippo Vaughn
283. Milt Pappas
284. Bill Gullickson
285. Steve Carlton
286. Larry Jackson
287. Wes Ferrell
288. Mike Scott
289. Joe and Phil Niekro
290. Todd Hundley
291. Frank Lary
292. Tris Speaker
293. Lou Gehrig, Harmon Killebrew
294. Doc White
295. John Hiller
296. Dan Quisenberry
297. Yogi Berra, father of Dale
298. Lee Smith
299. Tommy Davis
300. Reggie Jackson
301. Red Ruffing
302. Johnny Vander Meer
303. Jim Kaat
304. Gaylord Perry
305. Bob Feller, 1946 Cleveland Indians
306. Harry Walker
307. Otis Nixon
308. Willie Mays
309. Tommy Byrne
310. Charlie Comiskey
311. Jim Abbott
312. Cliff Heathcoate
313. Virgil and Jesse Barnes
314. Gil Hodges
315. Rusty Staub
316. Al Oliver

317. Bob Watson
318. Jack Taylor
319. George Foster
320. Jeff Reardon: Expos, Twins, Red Sox
321. Terry Pendleton
322. Lou Brock
323. Randy Hundley
324. Robin Yount
325. Whitey Ford
326. Omar Moreno
327. Jack Morris
328. Hank Sauer
329. Al Worthington
330. Rob Murphy
331. Mark Davis
332. Cap Anson
333. Brady Anderson
334. Juan Samuel
335. Tiny Bonham
336. Gary Gaetti
337. Mickey Mantle
338. Jim Brewer
339. Ty Cobb
340. Catfish Hunter
341. Ron Perranoski
342. Mudcat Grant
343. Phil Niekro, 1979
344. Frank Tanana
345. Terry Steinbach
346. Herb Score
347. Roy Campanella
348. Cecil Cooper
349. Stan Coveleski: Cleveland and Washington
350. Richie Ashburn
351. Rod Carew
352. Tony Taylor
353. Lee May
354. Doyle Alexander
355. Gorman Thomas
356. Will White

357. Edd Roush
358. Elmer Flick
359. Smoky Joe Wood
360. Rube Marquard
361. Bill Terry
362. Burleigh Grimes
363. Ty Cobb, 1908
364. Jimmy Reese
365. Lew Fonseca
366. Larry Doyle
367. Smoky Burgess
368. Ted Williams
369. Andre Dawson
370. Bob Johnson
371. Frank Robinson
372. Harmon Killebrew
373. Louisiana
374. Roger Maris
375. Ivan Rodriguez
376. Billy Pierce
377. Eddie Mulligan
378. Pete Rose
379. Julio Franco
380. Fergie Jenkins
381. Hack Wilson
382. Joe Morgan
383. Honus Wagner
384. Boston Braves
385. Warren Spahn
386. Robin Roberts
387. Zack Wheat
388. Reggie Jackson
389. Joe Cronin
390. Juan Marichal
391. Ralph Kiner
392. Lefty Gomez
393. Hank Aaron
394. Nap Lajoie
395. Hoyt Wilhelm
396. Sam Rice
397. George Sisler
398. Duke Snider

399. George Kell

400. Christy Mathewson

401. Ed Walsh

402. Mel Ott

403. Jimmie Foxx

404. Steve Carlton

405. Graig Nettles

406. Jimmy Collins

407. Darrell Evans

408. Felix Mantilla

409. Philadelphia A's

410. Satchel Paige

411. Mets, 1962

412. Gabby Hartnett

413. Cleveland Indians

414. John Clarkson

415. Tom Seaver, Phil Niekro

416. Tommy John

417. Ellie Hendricks

418. Dave Parker

419. Brooks Robinson

420. Dolf Luque

421. Warren Cromartie

422. Rafael Palmero

423. Joe Judge

424. Dave Kingman: Mets, Padres, Angels, Yankees

425. Jose Oquendo

426. Maury Wills

427. Wes Ferrell

428. Don Drysdale

429. Bobby Bonds

430. Joe Carter

431. Frank Howard

432. George Foster

433. Reggie Jackson

434. Phil Niekro

435. Mel Ott

436. Lloyd Waner

437. Early Wynn

438. Dwight Evans

439. Grover Alexander

440. Lou Gehrig

441. Carl Yastrzemski

442. Vinny Castilla

443. Billy Williams

444. Jim Rice

445. Ty Cobb

446. Three Finger Brown

447. Rabbit Maranville

448. Willie Keeler

449. Miller Huggins

450. Herb Pennock

451. Bob Feller

452. Ted Kluszewski

453. Stan Musial

454. Eddie Murray

455. Bill Dickey

456. Christy Mathewson

457. George Brett

458. Hank Aaron

459. Joe Sewell

460. Yogi Berra

461. Earl Averill

462. Eddie Collins

463. Connie Mack

464. Cal Ripken

465. Bobby Doerr

466. Rick Ferrell

467. Sherm Lollar

468. Ted Lyons

469. Jesse Burkett

470. Hoss Radbourn

471. Gaylord Perry

472. Kiki Cuyler

473. Roger Maris

474. Bill Nicholson

475. Chicago Cubs

476. Heinie Manush

477. Enos Slaughter

478. Wade Boggs

479. Dizzy Dean

480. Chuck Klein
481. 39
482. Ted Williams
483. Bill Buckner
484. Luis Aparicio
485. Earle Combs

486. Robin Yount
487. Rod Carew
488. Rico Petrocelli
489. Bill Terry
490. Rickey Henderson
491. Ray Chapman

CHAPTER NINE: TRADES

1. Sparky Adams
2. J. T. Snow
3. Rick Aguilera
4. John Smoltz
5. Tommy John
6. Joe Carter
7. Francisco Estrada, Leroy Stanton, and Don Rose
8. Earl Averill
9. Bobby Avila
10. Jackie Robinson
11. Jeff Bagwell
12. Dave Bancroft
13. Mort Cooper
14. Bobby Bonilla
15. Ryne Sandberg
16. Ken Boyer
17. Lew Burdette
18. Amos Rusie
19. Jeff Burroughs
20. Dolf Camilli
21. Rico Carty
22. Denny McLain
23. Cecil Cooper
24. Stan Coveleski
25. Zoilo Versalles
26. Mark Davis
27. Mike Marshall
28. Ted Sizemore
29. Larry Doby
30. Steve Carlton, Dennis Eckersley
31. Bobby Bonds
32. Gil Hodges

33. Jay Buhner
34. Pete Rose
35. Tom Seaver
36. Rube Marquard
37. Lloyd Waner
38. Johnny Mize
39. Eppa Rixey
40. Eddie Plank
41. Ernie Lombardi
42. Bill McKechnie, Christy Mathewson, Edd Roush
43. Pete Runnels
44. Vida Blue
45. Jackie Jensen
46. George Case
47. Claudell Washington
48. Earl Webb
49. Hoyt Wilhelm
50. Billy Williams
51. Stan Williams
52. Maury Wills
53. Rudy York
54. Joaquin Andujar
55. Andre Dawson
56. Roger Maris
57. Mike Cuellar
58. Joe Adcock
59. Lou Brock
60. Norm Cash
61. Dave Magadan
62. George Foster
63. Lou Pinella
64. Amos Otis

65. Allie Reynolds
66. Chick Hafey
67. Chuck Klein
68. Joe Jackson
69. George Kell
70. Herb Score
71. Joe Cronin
72. Al Lopez
73. Ron Santo
74. Willie Mays
75. Sparky Lyle
76. Mike McCormick
77. Willie McGee
78. Jose Mesa
79. Pedro Guerrero
80. Brady Anderson
81. Red Ruffing
82. Roy Sievers

83. Goose Goslin
84. Don Baylor
85. Joe Carter
86. Chuck Tanner
87. Nellie Fox
88. Gaylord Perry
89. Jim Bunning
90. Jeff Reardon
91. Arky Vaughan
92. Tris Speaker
93. Dazzy Vance
94. Tom Brunansky
95. Bob Welch
96. Rick and Wes Ferrell
97. Dave Winfield
98. John Mayberry
99. Cy Young
100. Dizzy Dean

CHAPTER TEN: NATIONAL ASSOCIATION

1. Al Spalding
2. Harry Wright
3. Dick McBride
4. Cap Anson
5. Andy Leonard
6. New York, Philadelphia, and Boston

7. Pud Galvin
8. Troy
9. Bob Ferguson
10. Rynie Wolters

CHAPTER ELEVEN: NEGRO LEAGUES

1. Larry Doby, Monte Irvin
2. Lyman Bostock
3. James
4. Ernie Banks
5. Willie Wells
6. Ray Dandridge
7. Satchel Paige
8. K.C. Monarchs
9. Oscar Charleston
10. Leon Day

11. Roy Campanella
12. Birmingham Black Barons
13. Martin Dihigo
14. Josh Gibson
15. John Henry Lloyd
16. Buck Leonard
17. Judy Johnson
18. Rube and Willie Foster
19. Luis Tiant Sr.
20. Buck O'Neil

CHAPTER TWELVE: THE WORLD SERIES AND CHAMPIONSHIP PLAYOFFS

1. Lefty Grove
2. Possum Whitted
3. Bob Welch
4. Babe Ruth, 1918
5. Vic Davalillo
6. 1955
7. Danny Murphy
8. Art Ditmar, 1960
9. Lance Johnson
10. George Hendrick, Angel Mangual
11. Frank Crosetti
12. Dennis Martinez
13. Don Gullett
14. Heinie Zimmerman
15. Buddy Myer
16. Don Baylor
17. Wally Schang
18. 1918
19. Chief Bender
20. Jimmy Sebring, Chick Stahl
21. Fred Clarke
22. Ted Kluszewski
23. Eddie Plank
24. Larry Andersen
25. George Pipgras
26. Graig Nettles
27. Dave Concepcion
28. Three Finger Brown
29. Honus Wagner
30. Fred Lindstrom
31. Mickey Lolich, Bob Gibson
32. Monte Pearson
33. Jesse Orosco
34. Les Straker
35. Mike Torrez
36. Chick Hafey
37. Deacon Phillippe
38. Allie Reynolds
39. Billy Hatcher
40. Bruce Kison
41. Mike Davis
42. Warren Spahn
43. Johnny Kucks
44. Darold Knowles
45. Tony Pena
46. Juan Marichal, Gaylord Perry
47. Don Newcombe
48. Danny Jackson
49. Scott Garrelts
50. Bob Kuzava
51. Will McEnaney
52. Jim Beattie
53. Doyle Alexander
54. Jim Palmer
55. Dave Winfield
56. Goose Goslin
57. Gene Tenace
58. Joe Gibbon
59. .186 (1918 Red Sox)
60. Yankees, 1960
61. Red Rolfe
62. Babe Ruth
63. Doug Drabek
64. Mark Littel
65. Ginger Beaumont
66. Jim Bagby
67. Pat Dobson
68. Joe Tinker
69. Tommy Jefferson Davis Bridges
70. Bill Abstein
71. Ray Noble
72. Milt Wilcox
73. Don Hoak
74. Fernando Valenzuela
75. Richie Hebner
76. Pete Mikkelsen
77. John Miljus
78. Johnny Podres
79. Jeff Leonard
80. Fred Toney
81. Stan Coveleski

82. Joe Sewell
83. Bill Wambsganss
84. New York Giants 1921–22
85. Chicago Cubs, White Sox, 1906
86. Andruw Jones
87. Danny Jackson: Kansas City, Cincinnati, Pittsburgh, Philadelphia, St. Louis
88. Will Clark, Mark Grace
89. George Brett
90. Tony Castillo
91. Don Drysdale, 13–16, 1966
92. 1985
93. Carl Mays
94. Ross Grimsley
95. Vic Wertz
96. Willie Horton
97. Joe DiMaggio
98. St. Louis Cardinals
99. Rube Marquard
100. Jessie Haines
101. Charlie Leibrandt
102. Vic Lombardi
103. Bobby Cox
104. Reds, 1976
105. Marquis Grissom
106. John Wetteland
107. Dennis Eckersley
108. Al Smith
109. Jimmy Key
110. David Wells
111. Red Ruffing, Paul Derringer
112. George Frazier
113. Johnny Sturm
114. Whitey Kurowski
115. Pee Wee Reese
116. Moe Drabowsky
117. Bob Miller
118. Bob Feller
119. Joe Jackson
120. Harry Hooper

121. Johnny Evers
122. Walter Johnson
123. Johnny Bench, Thurman Munson
124. Curt Schilling
125. Travis Jackson
126. Frank Demaree
127. Frank Frisch
128. Bill Voiselle
129. Lefty Williams
130. Joe Medwick
131. Phil Garner
132. Billy Martin
133. Vic Wertz
134. Phillies, 1950
135. Hank Borowy
136. Jose Santiago
137. Bert Blyleven
138. Jim Palmer
139. Mark Koenig
140. Chris Sabo
141. Steve Garvey
142. Bobby Richardson
143. Brooklyn, 1920
144. Gil Hodges
145. Fred Schulte
146. Babe Ruth, Carl Mays
147. Max Lanier
148. Jim Kaat
149. Pinky Higgins
150. Elston Howard
151. Marv Owen
152. Burleigh Grimes
153. Dave Stewart
154. Vic Willis
155. Cincinnati Reds
156. Jerry Koosman
157. Sal Maglie
158. Jack Coombs, Chief Bender
159. Charlie Keller
160. Johnny Logan

CHAPTER THIRTEEN: ALL-STAR GAMES

1. Lefty Gomez
2. Ken Raffensberger
3. 1969, RFK Stadium in Washington
4. Dwight Gooden
5. Frank Robinson, Johnny Bench, Hank Aaron, Roberto Clemente, Reggie Jackson, Harmon Killebrew
6. Robin Roberts
7. The Griffeys
8. White Sox, Frank Thomas
9. J. R. Richard
10. Tyler Green
11. Jack Armstrong
12. Gary Sheffield
13. Steve Garvey, Jimmy Wynn
14. Tim Raines
15. Dave Stenhouse
16. Steve Ontiveros
17. Rick Dempsey, 24 years
18. Paul Derringer
19. Luis Tiant, Don Drysdale
20. Johnny Mize

CHAPTER FOURTEEN: ALL-AMERICAN GIRLS PROFESSIONAL BASEBALL LEAGUE

1. Illinois, Indiana
2. Jimmie Foxx
3. Max Carey
4. Milwaukee
5. 40 feet

CHAPTER FIFTEEN: APPENDICES

1. Nine balls for a walk
2. Walks were counted as hits. However, the statistics have since been adjusted to reflect the current rule.
3. The pitching mound was moved to its current distance of 60'6" from home plate.
4. Runners were credited with a steal for every additional base advanced on a hit or an out.
5. Only the winning run counted, and the hit was downgraded.
6. They had less than 502 plate appearances.
7. Spitball
8. Pitchers needed to throw at least 10 complete games, and Maddux was two shy.
9. Game-Winning RBI
10. Combined efforts, less than nine innings, and broken up in extra innings